INVOLVING PARENTS IN NURSERY AND INFANT SCHOOLS

THE
HIGH/SCOPE
PRESS
a division of
High/Scope Educational Research Foundation
600 North River Street
Ypsilanti, MI 48197
(313) 485-2000

First published in England (1981) by
Grant McIntyre, Ltd., London

Library of Congress Cataloging in
Publication Data

Tizard, Barbara.
   Involving parents in nursery and infant
   schools.
   Reprint. Originally published: London: Grant
   McIntyre, 1981.
   Includes indexes.
   1. Nursery schools—England. 2. Education,
   Preschool—England. 3. Parent-teacher
   relationships. I. Mortimore, Jo. II. Burchell,
   Bebb. III. Title.

   LB1140.25.G7T59   1983
   372.11'03   83-10656

   ISBN 0-931114-18-7

Printed in the United States of America

Involving Parents in Nursery and Infant Schools:

a source book for teachers

Barbara Tizard, Jo Mortimore and
Bebb Burchell

High
Scope
Press

Foreword to the American Edition

Involving Parents in Nursery and Infant Schools, which is based upon experience in England, also has some important things to say to early educators in the United States. From the first chapter titled "Why Involve Parents?" to the last, "Involving Parents from Minority Groups," the authors address a series of practical issues set in the rational framework of their extended research study. Every educator in the United States who is interested in parent involvement has faced these or similar issues.

With refreshing frankness, the authors examine the origin of the present parent involvement trend and the reluctance of many educators to go further in parent involvement than to arrange meetings in which teachers "inform" parents. Numerous examples of the differences between parents' and teachers' perceptions of schools and of parent involvement in the schools both enliven the text and illuminate the problems that separate the two groups.

For Tizard, Mortimore and Burchell, parent involvement is not an either/or issue. They explore numerous ways, ranging from preschool clubs to parents as authors, in which parents can be more closely associated with the schools their children attend. These explorations are strengthened by the findings of the authors' extended intervention study in which they helped seven nursery schools design and use strategies for involving parents. The seven schools in the intervention study served families from a broad range of social, economic and language backgrounds.

In an especially useful chapter, "Some Underlying Difficulties," the authors discuss several problems which their experience tells them get in the way of parent involvement. Lack of resources, communication difficulties, and teachers' and parents' beliefs in professionalism, all are viewed as hindering attempts at parent involvement. In recent years, "communication gap" has become a sort of education buzz word, devoid of substance. But when the authors of *Involving Parents in Nursery and Infant Schools* use the expression, they attach significant meaning to it, as when they talk about working with parents from a different culture and say that communication problems may arise "... because not only some of their values, but also their conceptions of childhood, parenthood, play, toys and schooling, are likely to differ." (p. 102) They then describe enough about these sources of dissimilarities that the interested reader can immediately understand the nature of the communication gap.

Unlike the recommendations in many books, those contained in this book are not simple suggestions derived directly from the research. Instead, each one is a complex, complete model built around a unitary concept. Readers will find that each recommendation concludes with a brief section on how to determine the success of the suggestion and gain information to guide improvement.

Some pronounced differences exist in the parent involvement issues faced by educators in England and in the United States. For example, "minority group" in England has a more restricted functional meaning than it does in the United States. Some words are different also—outing (field trip), tick (check off), crèche (nursery). But the similarities far outweigh the differences, and the insights gained are universal: "One useful approach to this problem [poor attendance at parent meetings] is to consider whether there is something wrong with the meetings rather than the parents."

Involving Parents in Nursery and Infant Schools is a joy to read. The images are vivid and the prose is excellent. Teachers, parents, administrators and policy makers all will find material of interest in this book. They will receive the added benefit that comes from reading a thoughtful and well-written treatise on a topic of consuming social interest in this half of the twentieth century.

—*Robert L. Egbert*
Professor of Education
University of Nebraska—Lincoln
May 1983

Contents

Contents

Acknowledgements

This study was made possible by a grant from the Department of Education and Science, and by the collaboration of the parents, head teachers, class teachers, nursery assistants and nursery advisors of the seven schools which took part in the project. We are grateful to these teachers for their comments on this book, and for the comments of Ann Brackenbridge, Margaret Moss and Joyce Watt. Our thanks are also due to Mrs. K. Culbard for patiently and efficiently typing several drafts of the manuscript.

The section on involving parents in the teaching of reading (pages 197–206) was contributed by a colleague in the Thomas Coram Research Unit, Jenny Hewison. The project of involving parents in writing books for their children (pages 194–7) was carried out by Heather Sutton, a member of the research team during its second year.

Nine tables, which present the findings reported here in greater detail, have been deposited with the British Library, Lending Division, Boston Spa, Wetherby, West Yorkshire LS23 7BQ, where they may be inspected.

Part I

Issues and research findings

I

Why involve parents?

What is parent involvement?

In 1975 the Department of Education asked one of the authors (Barbara Tizard) to put forward a research proposal concerned with parent involvement in nursery education. The proposal was approved and the research which gave rise to this book was carried out between 1976 and 1979.

In the first part of this book we describe how we carried out our project, what questions we tried to answer, and what our findings were. In the second part, we offer detailed suggestions about methods of involving parents in schools. We go on to analyse some of the underlying difficulties in putting parent involvement into practice, and on the basis of our work we make some policy recommendations.

But before describing our own research it seems important that we set it in the context of current educational thinking. What is meant by parent involvement? Why did the Department of Education select this topic as a priority for research investigation? And why, indeed, were we sufficiently convinced of its importance to commit three years to its study?

Parent involvement was in the air in the seventies. Organized groups of parents, the Pre-school Playgroup Association, and most educationalists and teachers in the nursery and infant sector agreed that it was important. Yet even a brief discussion of the topic disclosed doubts, conflicts, and reservations. The most enthusiastic advocates seemed to be furthest from the coal face. Educational theorists, advisors and inspectors tended to be more convinced of the need to involve parents than did heads and teachers, while parents often failed to respond when teachers did attempt to involve them.

It soon became clear that any discussion of parent involvement was hindered by lack of consensus on the meaning of the term. To some teachers, it meant the active presence of parents within the school, helping in the classroom, mending and making equipment, using parents' rooms. To others, it implied that parents were involved in the management and decision-making processes of the school. Still others meant little more by the term than that parents were energetic and generous in raising funds for the school, conscientious in their attendance at open days and social events, and friendly in their relationships with the staff. Psychologists, on the other hand, tended to use the term to refer to planned attempts to involve parents in educational activities with their children.

Confusion is caused not only by these differences in interpretation, but by the fact that parent involvement is advocated for a variety of unconnected reasons. This emerges as soon as one asks, Whom is it intended to benefit? And in what way? Is it intended to benefit the teachers—by providing them with volunteer help, or by adding to their understanding of their pupils? The parents—by enriching their relationship with their children, or by giving them the opportunity to increase their influence and control over the schools? The children—by raising their IQs and educational achievements, or by ensuring greater harmony and understanding between home and school?

Parent involvement is nowadays such an acceptable aim for a school that its desirability tends to be assumed, and these questions are not always answered, or even asked. Yet teachers are often uneasily aware that parents' reasons for advocating increased involvement may differ from their own. A head teacher, for example, who successfully mobilizes numbers of parents to help in the school may be careful to see that no

4

parents' association is formed, lest parents try to 'take over' from him.

Despite these differences in the meaning given to the term, and the motivations for advocating it, most advocates of parent involvement share one belief—*that the relationship between home and school should be changed in such a way that parents take a more active role than was formerly the case in their children's education.* The question which will be discussed in this chapter is why this belief emerged as an important educational issue in the sixties. It will be argued that its emergence was the result of a number of nearly simultaneous but distinct developments in both psychological and socio-political thinking. In consequence, pressure to change home-school relationships came from several different quarters, with the resultant confusion of meanings and reasons which we have described.

Home-school relationships before the sixties

Traditionally, parents were not assigned a role within the school. More than that, they were usually physically excluded except on formal occasions such as open days. In the private sector of education this exclusion was usually set in a context of mutual trust and support. The parent had generally chosen the school precisely because he wanted for his child what the school had to offer; he shared the school's values, and was prepared to back the teacher up to the best of his ability. Home and school, although separate worlds, were in harmony.

This was rarely the case in the public sector. Parents were not expected to choose a school for their child, and often were not accorded common courtesy: notices stipulating NO PARENTS PAST THIS POINT were not uncommon in state schools until the sixties. In many schools, parents were only summoned for a private discussion when their children were in trouble. Equally, the staff could not rely on the back-up from the parents they would wish. Mutual understanding and shared values could not be assumed. Because of this, while teachers did not expect parents to play a role within the school, in the state primary system, they did attempt to influence what went on at home. Their attempts were mainly directed towards the moral and physical welfare of their pupils. These were presented in successive editions of an official handbook for teachers, *Suggestions for the Consideration of Teachers and Others Concerned in the Work of Public and Elementary Schools*. The first edition, published in 1905, urged schools to impress their values on the home. 'Much of the moral shipwreck of young people can be traced to parental ignorance or neglect. . . . Managers and education authorities can promote the moral no less than the physical and intellectual well-being of the scholars . . . if they can only induce parents to resume control of their children.'

In order to be given advice, parents must be in touch with teachers. Hence some schools developed structures for this purpose, for instance, issuing invitations to parents to attend medical inspections when they could be advised, and setting up parents' associations, where talks were given by teachers and doctors. The Hadow Report on Nursery and Infant Schools (1931) noted that a large number of these associations had been set up, and 'as a result of effective cooperation between parents, doctors and school nurses, there has been a marked improvement alike in the health and cleanliness of the children, in the character of their clothing, and the hygiene of the home' (page 96).

These parents' associations originated in the nursery sector of education. Perhaps because of the influence of Margaret McMillan (see pages 28–30), parents were often encouraged to play a larger role in nursery schools than elsewhere in the educational system. The Hadow Report stated that some nursery schools had open days when parents could watch the daily round of school activities. 'The gratitude of the parents is displayed in many ways, for instance mothers help in washing school linen and overalls, and fathers construct toys, and attend

to the garden' (page 105). The staff-parent relationship depicted in the Report as ideal has, in fact, a distinctly Victorian
flavour—teachers dispense advice to ignorant but grateful
working people.

By the late forties, however, because of the improvement in
the standard of living of the British working class that took place
during and after the Second World War, attempts to advise
parents on health and diet were largely abandoned. It was
recognized that children were generally receiving good physical
care at home; the concern of educationalists was now directed
more to the emotional needs of young children. Because of the
influence of psychoanalysts such as John Bowlby (1951), the
age of admission to nursery school was raised from two to three
years, and children were offered either a morning or an afternoon session, rather than all-day attendance. Mothers' clubs
disappeared from nursery and infant schools. By 1959 the
Ministry of Education *Recommendations for Primary Schools* no
longer had a special home-school section. Parent education and
other methods of influencing parents were not mentioned. Instead, the emotional bond between mother and child was emphasized in the advice to encourage mothers to stay with their
children until they were 'settled' into nursery school. In the
single other reference to parents it was said that 'mothers should
always be welcome in the school and a child should see his
mother and teacher in a friendly relationship'. Yet only eight
years later one of the main messages of the Plowden Report
(1967) was that 'one of the essentials for educational advance is
a closer partnership between the two parties to every child's
education'. What was responsible for this change in official
thinking?

The present interest in parent involvement

1 The rise of environmental theories of intelligence and
   egalitarian political beliefs

The dominant belief in British educational circles for many
years, enshrined in the writings of Cyril Burt, was that educational achievement was in the main dependent on genetic
intellectual endowment. Most children were destined to be
hewers of wood; not only was this seen as inevitable, but by
many also as desirable. The sentiments of the hymn, 'The rich
man in his castle, the poor man at his gate, God made them high
or lowly, and ordered their estate' expressed a view of society
that was held widely until the Second World War.

In the post-war period genetic theories of intelligence were
gradually replaced by environmental ones, and more egalitarian political beliefs prevailed. Thus by 1963 a Conservative
Minister of Education, Sir Edward Boyle, could write 'All
children should have an equal opportunity of acquiring intelligence, and of developing their talents and abilities to the full'
(Newsom, 1963). However, during the fifties and sixties a series
of research reports revealed not only a marked association
between parental occupation and children's measured intelligence and educational achievements, but also that the educational achievements of working class children lagged behind
those of middle class children of the same IQ (*Early Leaving*,
1954; the Crowther Report, 1959; Douglas, 1964). As the
children grew older, this gap increased; it was clear that the
reforms introduced by the 1944 Education Act had not succeeded in ensuring the full development of working class
children's abilities.

Concern over the wastage of talent revealed by these reports
was one of the main spurs to the development of interest in
parent involvement. Educationalists began to search for the
factors in the background of working class children that were
responsible for their under-achievement.

a *Equalizing opportunity by increasing parental knowledge of education.*
Interviews with working class parents have consistently shown
that they tend to have much less knowledge of the educational
system, and of school practices, than middle class parents, and
that they are usually very conscious of their ignorance. Jackson
and Marsden (1962), in a detailed study of middle class and
working class families whose children had attended grammar
school, found many examples of this ignorance. For example,
the middle class parents knew how to set about choosing primary and secondary schools with good academic records while
working class parents, lacking this knowledge, made these decisions on trivial grounds. At a later stage 'they knew so little—
not even the vocabulary of higher education . . . that they often
lacked the raw material to ask questions with.'

In a study of the working class parents of junior school
children, Young and McGeeney (1968) found a good deal of
ignorance about the general organization of the school, and of
the methods in use. 'Even the tiniest difference in arithmetic
methods since the parents were at school could be a source of
confusion. . . . They could see the massive walls; they did not
understand what went on behind them.'

Jackson and Marsden pointed out that in these circumstances a ten-minute annual interview with the teacher was a
stupendously inadequate communication channel. They suggested 'better by far to give the children a week's extra holiday,
but let the teachers be on duty all afternoon and evening for
parents to come up, and come up more than once'. Eric Midwinter was later to echo the view that much of the disadvantage
of working class children at school is due to their parents' lack of
educational know-how. He argued that there was an urgent
need to sell education to the parents—'in essence, a monu-
mental public relations task faces all teachers' (1977).

b *Equalizing opportunity by increasing parental interest in education.* A
more widely held view was that the working class child was
disadvantaged at school because his parents lacked interest in

his educational progress. This view seemed to be supported by the findings of the National Survey of Health and Development, which followed the development of all children born in Britain in one week of March, 1946 (Douglas, 1964). The survey showed that the most powerful factor affecting educational achievement at both eight and eleven years of age was the level of parental interest—the effects of social class, size of family, quality of housing, and the academic record of the school were all smaller. The effect of parental interest could partly be explained by its relation to social class—a larger proportion of middle class than working class children had very interested parents. But *within* each social class, the children who had very interested parents scored higher on achievement tests than those with uninterested parents. Assessment of the level of parental interest was based in this study on the judgement of the class teachers, and the records of the number of times the parents had visited the schools to discuss their child's progress.

From these findings it was a small step to the conclusion that if only more working class parents would interest themselves in their children's education, equality of educational opportunity might become a reality. Douglas himself did not take this step but the Plowden Report on primary education did (1967). The Plowden Committee commissioned their own large survey of primary school children, teachers and parents, and found, like Douglas, that parental attitudes to school were more strongly associated with high educational achievement than any other factor. They concluded that 'a strengthening of parental encouragement may produce better performance in school', and urged teachers to devise means for increasing parental participation in education. 'It has long been recognized that education is concerned with the whole man: henceforth it must be concerned with the whole family' (page 5).

This conclusion did not meet with universal agreement; not everyone accepted that there was good evidence for the belief that increasing parental participation in school *would* increase educational achievement. The Plowden survey had certainly established a strong relationship between parental attitudes and educational achievement. But the measure of parental attitudes used in their analysis was composed of answers to questions as diverse as whether the parents had taken recreational courses, whether the family went on outings together, whether the father had visited the child's school, whether the parents hoped the child would go to a grammar school, whether the child talked to the parents about school, the library membership of parents and children, the number of books at home, as well as the frequency of parents' contacts with school.

While answers to these questions might reasonably be regarded as reflecting parents' attitudes to education, and seem likely to relate to the level of the child's school achievement, they go far beyond the narrower issue of the parents' interest in the school. Bernstein and Davies (1969) argued that the Plowden measure of parental attitudes was in fact a measure of strongly class-linked behaviour patterns, and it was these behaviour patterns that were associated with school achievement. Hence encouraging schools to increase their contacts with parents could not in itself be expected to raise the achievement of working class children.

Throughout the Plowden report there is an assumption that the frequency of parental contacts with school is a good measure of parental interest. Yet their own survey contained good evidence that working class parents *were* interested in their children's education, even though they made fewer visits to school than middle class parents. Seventy-three per cent of parents in the top infant class (six to seven year olds) were helping them with school work. There was remarkably little social class difference in the proportion of parents who wanted their children to be given homework—professional class, 64 per cent; skilled and semi-skilled manual workers, both 60 per cent; unskilled workers, 54 per cent. Seventy-five per cent of skilled manual workers wanted their children to stay on at school after the minimum leaving age, as did 64 per cent of unskilled workers (Plowden, volume 2, 1967). Ten years later, John and

Elizabeth Newson found that 82 per cent of Nottingham working class parents of seven year olds helped them with reading (1977).

This evidence suggests that whatever the reason for the lower educational achievements of working class children, it is not lack of interest on the part of their parents. This was also the opinion of Jackson and Marsden, who found that despite the anxiety of working class parents for their children to do well at school they made only sporadic contacts with the staff (1962). After discussing this issue with the parents, they concluded that the parents felt the school to be particularly alien, and considered that the comments and advice they received from the teachers when they did contact them were unhelpful and uninformative.

But by the late sixties, the arguments that equality of opportunity could be realized by giving parents more information about education, or encouraging them to make more contacts with school, both began to lose plausibility. This was because new research findings suggested that the roots of educational failure would not be so easily eradicated.

c *Equalizing opportunity by influencing mother-child interaction.* During the sixties, a number of studies were published which suggested that the low educational achievement of working class children had a more profound cause than their parents' lack of knowledge about or interest in school. The problem was seen to lie rather in the characteristics of their intellectual functioning, which made it difficult for them to meet the academic demands of school. The crude formulation of this theory was that 'disadvantaged' children are under-stimulated at home, especially linguistically, with the result that their grasp of language is deficient. This view was endorsed in the Bullock Report *A Language for Life* (1975), which quoted with approval the advice of a health visitor to expectant mothers 'When you give your child a bath, bathe him in language.' Children in deprived areas are often said to arrive at school barely able to speak, and lacking a knowledge of basic concepts.

There is good reason to believe that this view is something of a myth. A small minority of children may suffer grave deprivation, but there is considerable evidence that the great majority of young working class children both talk and are talked to a great deal at home (e.g. Wootton, 1974; Tizard *et al.*, 1980). By the time they start school, most have a sufficient grasp of language structures and usage to undertake the task of reading (Francis, 1974).

This is not to say that there are not social class differences in children's intellectual functioning, nor in the ease with which they tackle school work. The best known formulation of these differences is Bernstein's (1971). Although he is often incorrectly said to believe that working class children are linguistically deprived, in fact he considers them to have the same knowledge of language structure and usage as middle class children. He sees social class differences rather in the greater facility of middle class children to give and to understand universalistic meanings, that is, meanings not bound to a specific context. This facility is related to the greater tendency of middle class mothers when talking to their children to discuss specific acts and events in relation to general principles, reasons and consequences. Since school is essentially concerned with the study of ideas, objects and events out of context, and with the transmission of general principles, working class children are at a disadvantage in the school setting (1970).

Variants of this theory were later advanced by other authors, all of whom stressed the global nature of working class children's intellectual disadvantage (for instance, Bruner, 1974; Blank, 1973; Tough, 1976). The problem was not thought to be that the children lacked specific skills, suffered from a restricted vocabulary, or had not learnt to use language in complex ways. It was rather that their inclination was to function at a more restricted intellectual level. 'The poorly functioning child will use his intellectual skills mainly when required to do so, while the well-functioning child will freely use them in a wide variety of situations. Development of any skill depends on its use . . . [it is this which] gives the well-functioning child a constant edge over his poorly functioning peer' (Blank, 1973).

The inference from these studies drawn by many education-alists (although not by the authors cited above) was that to raise the school achievements of working class children, it was neces-sary to alter the style of parent child interaction in working class homes. Parental involvement in education was therefore ad-vocated because it would provide opportunities for the staff to influence working class parents.

d *Equalizing opportunity: the need to intervene in the first five years of life.* An added impetus to the argument that parent involvement is needed in order to equalize educational opportunity was provided by the belief that the first five years is a crucial period of intellectual development. This was not a new belief (it can be traced back at least as far as Plato) but it became particularly prominent in the fifties and sixties because at this period re-search in three separate areas appeared to support it. Early mother-child relationships were said to be decisive for later mental health (Bowlby, 1951); a great deal of animal research suggested that imprinting, early stimulation, and other early experiences had permanent effects (see a review by Connolly, 1972); and longitudinal studies of children's IQs showed that IQ is quite variable in the early years, but becomes fairly stable by the age of four (Bloom, 1964). By this age, the IQ correlates about 0.7 with the IQ at age 17; this means that half of the variance in adult IQ can be predicted at the age of four.

This last finding was immediately misinterpreted to mean that 50 per cent of adult intelligence is developed by the age of four—a misinterpretation which is still widespread. In fact, as Jensen pointed out, such a conclusion does not follow from knowing the size of the correlation. 'The correlation between height at age four and at age 17 is also about 0.7, but who would claim that half the adult height is attained by age four? . . . [this would mean that] the average four year old should grow up to be 6ft 7ins by age 17!' (Jensen, 1969).

Despite the considerable scepticism of some authors (especially Clarke and Clarke, 1976) it became generally accepted that a child's future is decisively shaped in the first few years of life. Since this is the period when parental influence is paramount, most advocates of parent involvement have stressed its especial importance in the nursery school.

e *Equalizing opportunity by altering the relationship between school and community.* A very different argument for involving parents in schools has been that it would reduce the alienation between home and school in deprived areas. The major British exponents of this view were A. H. Halsey, the National Director of the Educational Priority Area (EPA)* Research Project, 1968–71, and Eric Midwinter, its Liverpool director. The EPA project was an action research project, set up in the wake of the Plowden Report. Five teams worked independently in Birmingham, Dundee, Liverpool, London and Yorkshire, with the general aim of finding how best to raise educational standards in primary schools in EPAs.

Halsey and Midwinter argued that an important factor contributing to the low educational achievements of working class children was the difference in values and life experience between staff and parents. Schools in deprived areas were trying to purvey an alien middle class culture, of no interest or relevance to the majority of children or their parents. The solution to this problem involved nothing less than a change in the nature of education, which should be concerned not simply with reading and mathematics attainments, but with equipping children 'with the knowledge and skills to cope with, give power over and in the end to transform the conditions of their local community' (Halsey, 1972). This goal required the transformation of schools into community schools. The concept of the community school was not new. It had been advanced in the Plowden

* EPAs were defined as areas where children are handicapped educationally by their home conditions.

Report, where it was defined as a school 'open beyond ordinary school hours for the use of children, their parents, and exceptionally for other members of the community' (page 44). The Plowden proposal was put forward as one way in which a school could inform and interest parents—'parents can be invited to the schools in the evenings to learn about its ways and to make things that would be useful for the school' (page 47), but it was also argued for on the grounds that the community was entitled to have access to the educational resources for which it paid.

The EPA project leaders, particularly Halsey and Midwinter, transformed this concept. They envisaged the community school as a focus for the neighbourhood, not so much because it made material resources available, but because it offered activities and experiences that would change the attitudes of teachers, parents and children both to education and to the local community. These schools would 'come to terms with the values of the community instead of opposing them', so that teacher, parent and child could work effectively together. Hence not only must parents learn more about school, but schools must understand the families and environments in which their children lived, and use this knowledge in their teaching. They believed that the community school needed a new curriculum, which was 'relevant' rather than academic, in touch with the child's own experiences, and drawing its resources for language, history, geography and so on from the community in which he lived. The case for a new, 'relevant', curriculum was both that it would engage the interest of children and parents in deprived areas, who were alienated by academic teaching, and that it would equip the children to understand and reform the grim social environment in which they lived.

Community education as envisaged by Halsey and Midwinter was not therefore solely concerned with raising the educational standards of working class children; it was also seen as a mechanism for urban regeneration. In order to bring this about, the traditional distinctions between teachers, parents and children would need to be changed, so that 'children may teach and teachers learn, as well as *vice versa*, and parents may do both'. In fact, the community school 'seeks almost to obliterate the boundary between school and community, to turn the community into a school, and the school into a community' (page 189).

Parent involvement in education was thus seen as crucial, not as a method of enabling parents to learn from the teacher, but as a way of establishing links between the school and the community, and enabling parents to make a unique contribution to the school.

These ideas were in principle very radical; in order to implement them, drastic changes in the school system would be needed. 'Obliterating the boundaries between school and the community', for example, seems to require something akin either to de-schooling, or to major shifts in roles within the school, with parents sharing their skills and knowledge with teachers as well as children.

In fact, the EPA teams do not seem to have worked out in any detail the implications of their ideas. In order to 'come to terms with the values of the community', one would have to start by defining in what ways the values of a particular community differed from those of the school. It would then be necessary to decide whether these differences constituted a barrier to educational achievement, or to good staff-parent relationships, and if so, what action should be taken.

For example, if it were the case that the community did not respect educational achievement, how could the school come to terms with this value difference *and* raise children's educational levels? Again, there might be other value differences which affected staff-parent relationships rather than academic achievement. There are communities in Britain where a sizeable proportion of the parents hold views which the school staff consider racist and sexist. What does coming to terms with the community's values mean in this situation?

These questions seemed to have been skated over in the EPA

Project. In his discussion of value differences between home and school, Halsey argued that 'the success of the middle class school is that it identifies with its environment: this could point the road for many an EPA school'. Immediately, however he followed this by the qualification that schools could not 're-inforce and perpetuate values and attitudes which would widely be regarded as undesirable'. He then concluded that 'we must set out in search of a constructive partnership between schools and parents even in the most deprived areas', thus side-stepping all the difficult issues raised above.

2 The growth of parent consumer groups

The pressures for parent involvement discussed so far have all had as their aim the improvement of educational attainment. They have also all assumed that the initiative for change should come from the teachers. A very different source of pressure has come from the parent consumer groups, such as the Advisory Centre for Education (ACE) founded in 1960, and the Confederation for the Advancement of State Education (CASE), founded in 1962. These organizations have based their arguments primarily on the right of parents to be informed and consulted about schools' aims and methods. This view carries no necessary implication that such consultation will improve children's educational attainments. The aim of these organizations is to alter *teachers'* rather than parents' attitudes.

Their major concern is that schools should give parents adequate information, consult them, and involve them in school management. *Where,* the magazine published by ACE, typically contains articles with such titles as 'How parents can get things changed in schools' and 'A register of parent campaigns'. CASE has published an 18 point Parents' Charter, mainly concerned with the kind of information parents should be given and the ways in which they should be consulted and represented.

As with most consumer groups, support tends to come primarily from middle class parents. It seems likely that an important reason for the development of these groups in the sixties was the growing trend for middle class parents to send their children to state schools. There they found themselves without the influence of parents in private schools—in the sense that the state school was not dependent on their patronage for its continuance—and often without the traditional forms of communication from staff—such as termly reports about their children.

Parents' organizations, like ACE and CASE, have only reached a small proportion of parents. But many more must have been influenced in their attitude to staff-parent relationships by the steady erosion of faith in traditional forms of authority, including the authority of professionals. Parents are less likely to accept that teachers 'know best' than was formerly the case. They are more ready to assert a claim that because of their own knowledge of, and interest in their children they should be able to play some role in their education and be consulted about decisions which affect them.

This willingness to challenge the teaching profession has complex social origins. The last 15 years have seen the growth of many new organizations prepared to assert the rights of the interests they represent—for example, women's groups and environmental groups. An increasing uneasiness has developed about the extent to which the general public has any control over the decisions made on its behalf, and there is a growing belief that public services and professionals should be held accountable to their clients. As Halsey has put it, we have moved into a world 'in which all social relations are increasingly subjected to the authority of negotiation' (unpublished manuscript, 1980). Trends of this kind have inevitably had an impact in the educational sphere. Many parents who would, in the past, have accepted the role of respectfully supporting the school are now prepared to campaign with teachers for more nursery schools, or against cuts to the educational services, and equally expect the teachers to listen to their point of view on curriculum or on school rules.

3 The influence of alternative, parent-run services

Another important factor influencing the demand for parental involvement in education has been the rapid growth during the sixties and seventies of parent-run playgroups and community nurseries. The impetus to this development was the dearth of state-maintained nursery schools and nurseries. In 1960 scattered groups of mothers, largely middle class, began to set up and run their own playgroups. These were later federated into a national organization, the Pre-school Playgroups Association (PPA). Playgroups, like nursery schools, offer children a wide variety of play materials in a free-play setting. Although they usually lack trained staff, good equipment and buildings, their great asset, at least when parent-run, is enthusiastic parent participation and management.* The community nurseries, which developed somewhat later in the seventies, were set up by parents who wanted to provide their children not only with social and play experiences, but also with exposure to an 'alternative' ideology; some made, for instance, explicit attempts to counter sexist and racist attitudes (Hughes *et al.*, 1980).

There are only a handful of community nurseries in Britain, but the playgroup movement is very extensive—in 1977 18.5 per cent of all children under five in England and Wales were attending a playgroup, compared with only 6.7 per cent in nursery schools and classes. The Pre-school Playgroups Association organizes its own training courses, and publishes its own periodicals and educational material. Thus a movement which started as a self-help group for a small number of middle class housewives now effectively challenges the state system, not only

---

* About half of British playgroups are run by parent committees, the rest by private persons, charities, and so on.

by providing a viable alternative system, but one which offers a much more extensive service.

The significance of the playgroup movement for the education system lies not only in its demonstration that a preschool service *can* be run by parents without professional help, but in its claim that because it is parent-managed and run it provides a *better* service. From the outset playgroups were seen as providing for the needs of both parents and children. The benefits of parent involvement were not seen in terms of later educational gain. Rather, it was argued that children benefited emotionally from the involvement of their parents, and from the fact that playgroup staff and parents worked closely together. This involvement was also thought to meet the needs of parents, and to increase the satisfaction of their lives.

Parents who have helped to run a playgroup often feel reluctant to be excluded from their children's education when they come to nursery class or primary school. They are therefore less likely to accept the passive role traditionally assigned to parents in the educational system.

Demand for involvement: a summary

A variety of relatively distinct but mutually reinforcing influences contributed to the growing acceptance in the sixties and seventies of the idea that parental involvement was an important educational aim. These influences arose from new trends in psychological theory, and from changes in political and social beliefs.

A major impetus to parent involvement stemmed from evidence of under-achievement among working class children, despite post-war educational reforms. The various explanations for this under-achievement offered by educationalists—working class ignorance about education, a lack of interest, or a restricted style of parent-child communication—were all seen as pointing to the need for parental involvement in school. A widely held belief in the crucial importance of the first five years suggested that parental involvement was particularly necessary in nursery education. A very different source of pressure was organized parents' groups. The growth of these groups probably resulted from the movement of middle class children into state schools, the unwillingness of some of their parents to accept an authoritarian teacher-parent relationship, and a more general belief that professionals should give an account of themselves to their clients. A third source of pressure for parent involvement was the success of the play-group movement, which demonstrated that parents could not only be involved in early education, but could run a preschool service.

In addition to these easily traceable influences, there were probably more pervasive influences acting on the general climate of opinion. For example, it was not only educationalists who stressed that society should be concerned with the whole family rather than the child. During the seventies, economists and psychiatrists also began to talk about 'Family income policy' and 'Family therapy' and to reject the notion that an individual should be considered as an economic or psycho-logical unit independent of the family context.

2

The official view

What kinds of parent involvement have been advocated in major British government reports and implemented in action research projects? To what extent have these methods been more generally adopted in the educational system, and what kinds of methods have aroused most opposition? Finally, is there any evidence that parent involvement activities achieve the ends for which they were intended?

The Plowden Report

The first government recommendations in the area of parent involvement were set out in the Plowden Report (1967). This put forward a minimum programme for schools which comprised:

  a A regular system for the head and the class teacher to meet parents before the child entered
  b Arrangements for more formal private talks, preferably twice a year
  c Open days to be held at times chosen to enable parents to attend
  d Booklets to be prepared by the school and given to parents to inform them in their choice of children's schools and as to how they are being educated
  e Written reports on children to be made at least once a year;

the children's work to be seen by parents
f Special efforts to be made to make contact with parents
who do not visit the schools.

It was also recommended that parents should be allowed to choose their children's primary schools whenever possible, and that they should be invited to take part in out-of-school activities in the evenings and during holidays.

Despite the frequent use in the Plowden Report of the terms 'partnership', 'participation' and 'involvement', which suggest radical changes in staff-parent relationships, these recommendations were by no means revolutionary. They amounted to little more than the suggestion that parents should be given the kind of information and choice of school that parents in the private sector already expect. Behind the recommendations seemed to lie the assumption that if these were introduced into the state system working class parents would respond by supporting the school in the same way that middle class parents support private schools.

Perhaps because Michael Young, one of the founders of the parents' organization, ACE, was on the committee, the Report stated that 'parents have a right to know what goes on in their children's schools'. But it was emphasized that the most important reason for making the recommendations was to raise educational standards.

The Educational Priority Area project

While the Plowden Report saw parent involvement mainly in terms of giving information, the EPA project programmes of 1968–71 covered a much wider field. The Red House team in Yorkshire were particularly concerned to influence parents with young children. They organized a home visiting programme in which an educational visitor taught parents about the learning potential of play and books, and also about their own importance in influencing their children's development. They also set up a nursery group, run by a trained teacher assisted by parents, and backed up by home visits from the teacher and by an evening discussion group for parents.

In Birmingham and London, home-school liaison teachers and school-based social workers were appointed in primary schools. In London attempts were also made to use primary schools as a base for organizing evening and weekend leisure activities for parents and children.

The Liverpool team devoted much of its efforts to developing methods of improving relationships between schools, parents, and the community. As well as the more traditional measures advocated by Plowden (such as open evenings and prospectuses), Eric Midwinter devised a variety of dramatic techniques by which the school could 'sell' itself to parents and the community (1972, 1977). School exhibitions were held in supermarkets, bingo halls, and holiday camps, infant classes were taught in the centre of department stores, where the public could watch them taking place, street processions were organized, and coachloads of pupils visited factory canteens and old people's clubs to demonstrate the work of the school.

Plowden had recommended twice-yearly interviews with parents; Midwinter urged that there should be some form of contact with parents of primary school children at least once a week. In addition he suggested that each school should have a public relations scheme, including for instance a weekly change of material in their permanent exhibition spot set up in a local shop or pub, a termly street procession, and an annual week devoted to 'selling' the school to the community.

Despite all these innovations, Halsey's suggestion that 'all concerned with education should share both teaching and learning roles' does not seem to have been realized in practice. The Red House team were very successful in recruiting parents to assist their nursery group teacher, but the teaching role assigned to parents was tightly defined by the teacher. In London, parent involvement in the classroom took the form of inviting parents to accompany primary school children on a rural studies project once a week. The Liverpool team made a more radical innovation. Parents were invited into primary schools to carry out joint projects with their children, for example in one school parents and children made 15-minute tape recordings about the street in which they lived. However, in discussing these projects Halsey specifically set out to reassure teachers that 'the parent's role in the classroom is more like the child's than like the teacher's' (page 135).

With a few exceptions this statement seems true generally of the role of parents in the EPA project. Although the project focused on relationships between the family, the school, and the community, the issue of decision-making within the school, and the accountability of the teachers to parents and the community, was not raised. Nor do the EPA project leaders appear to have consulted parents about the kind of education they wanted for their children or the role they themselves wished to play within the school. Because the parents responded enthusiastically to displays of music and drama, Midwinter and Halsey seemed to have assumed that they would prefer that their children should devote more time to these subjects at school. Our own interviews suggest that the reverse is the case; given the choice, working class parents are likely to opt overwhelmingly for a traditional academic curriculum.

The Bullock Report

The authors of the Bullock Report on language in schools, *A Language for Life* (1975), impressed by research reports of social class differences in parent-child interactions in the first year of life, advocated measures to influence parental behaviour. These included courses on language development for secondary school children, talks to antenatal clinics, home visitors to visit mothers with young children, and encouragement to parents to help in the infant and nursery school in non-academic ways.

They also suggested that staff might organize mothers' clubs, where the value of books could be discussed.

The Bullock Report placed little emphasis on information-giving or on involving parents in teaching, and none at all on consulting them. Parents were to be encouraged to borrow and buy children's books and read to their children, but not to teach them to read. It was acknowledged that some children *do* learn to read at home, but the danger of parents communicating anxiety to their children was stressed. In the end it was not recommended that parents should help with the teaching of reading, either at home or in school. There were also no recommendations that methods used in the school to teach reading should be explained or demonstrated to parents.

Parents as teachers: the Renfrewshire and Haringey projects

Two recent research projects have disregarded Bullock's cautions and enlisted parents to teach their children, operating from the home base. In a study in Haringey, a multi-racial working class district of London, Tizard, Hewison and Schofield found that teachers could enlist the cooperation of almost all parents of six to eight year olds in the teaching of reading (Hewison, 1981). Parents were visited at home five or six times a year, asked to hear their children read three or four times a week, and shown how to do this. A simple communication system between home and school was organized. The children who were helped at home had significantly higher reading attainments at the end of two years than either children whose parents were not involved in this way, or children who were given extra help in reading at school.

Donachy and Clark have also argued that the most effective form of parent involvement is for the teacher to enlist the help of the parent as a teacher operating in her own home (1979). Their study with the parents of three and four year old children in

Scotland required the mother to spend 30 minutes a day at home reading to her children from books supplied by the teacher, and carrying out a programme devised to develop concepts of time, space, size, etc. The children made substantial IQ gains over a four month period.

Margaret McMillan: a digression into history

Although the current widespread interest in parent involvement dated from the sixties, the first experiments in parent involvement took place at the beginning of the century.

In 1911 Margaret McMillan founded one of the first English nursery schools, in Deptford. The children for whom her school was started were malnourished, ragged and verminous, their parents burdened with extreme poverty, and often illiterate. Despite this, she sought to arouse their interest in education, and to encourage them to feel responsibility for the school. She pioneered many modern forms of parent involvement—families were visited at home, a parents' room was provided in the school, and parents were encouraged to spend as much time in school as they could.

Her views are of particular interest, because unlike most later exponents of parent involvement she raised the issue of parent control. She argued (McMillan, 1919) that just as wealthier mothers employ nurses to care for their children, but do not give up responsibility or control, so this should also be the case in nursery schools. 'And the working class mother, what of her nursery? To begin with, it would seem to be much more important to make her sovereign, if not ruler, of this new domain, rather than to assume at once that she can never be anything but an outsider. . . . A mother pays a small sum. In return, we take her child, and yet leave her the right to enter when she pleases, and to make suggestions, and even to give orders. There is only one thing she cannot do . . . and that is to dismiss the nurse-teachers. . . . The existing nursery schools are not yet controlled by the mothers of the children who attend them. But already parents' committees are being formed. Already too, it is clear to many that the nurseries must be built as an annexe to homes, and that as far as possible the homes should open on these child-gardens so as to make the frequent visits and constant oversight of mothers a possibility.'

Her conception of the role of the school in many ways anticipated the later community school movement. The school was to be the focus for adult education and recreation, where mothers could develop their latent abilities and find greater fulfilment. She started a weekly club with aims closer to those of an adult education class than a parents' association. 'It is not assumed that parents come to the club because they are ignorant, any more than it is believed that people go to religious services and lectures because they are ignorant or in special need of help.' The weekly club meetings were therefore seen not only as occasions to teach mothers useful skills such as dress making, but also as opportunities for them to become generally better informed. Famous people such as Bernard Shaw and Walter de la Mare were invited to speak on social and international affairs and the mothers were encouraged to take part in discussions 'in which they revealed . . . the arts, the wisdom, and also the hopes of the very poor'.

Unlike the EPA project leaders, Margaret McMillan (1908) linked the idea of the school as an adult education centre with the concept of parent control. 'If the people knew the schools well, were allies and friends of the teacher, understood and loved the methods by which their children were developing, if the school was their place for refreshment or entertainment, the bright spot of every area, do you think they would yield it up to the control of "Managers" and "Committees"?' She was also anxious that parents should be active as citizens. After the 1918 Education Act, which empowered but did not oblige local authorities to provide nursery schools for children between the ages of two and five, she urged parents to put pressure on their local authority to implement the Act.

Margaret McMillan's motivation for advocating parent involvement was political. Although she was concerned to raise children's educational achievements, she considered that to be the job of the teacher. As a Christian Socialist, she saw parent involvement as a way in which impoverished families could play a part in re-shaping their destinies and creating a new society. It was for this reason that she wanted parents to be accorded respect and even given control within the nurseries, helped to develop their abilities, and encouraged to take part in political activity.

These ideas were so far ahead of their time that few of them took root; most people remember Margaret McMillan only as the founder of the nursery school movement. Some of her ideas seem to have disappeared almost without trace until they were re-invented in the sixties and seventies—particularly the notion that mothers had the right to enter school when they pleased, and to take part in the management of the school, and that however ill-informed they were about education their views should be listened to with respect.

What *did* remain for many years was the tradition of mothers' circles attached to nursery schools—although they became a vehicle for advice to parents rather than an opportunity for adult education.

The response of the educational system

To what extent have the general run of primary schools responded to the pressure from government reports, research findings, and parents' groups to increase parent involvement? Unfortunately, no systematic documentation exists with which to answer this question, and it is only possible to piece together fragments of information and general impressions. Some forms of parent involvement seem to have been quite widely adopted, others have failed to interest, or have antagonized teachers.

1   Giving information to parents about schools

It seems likely that most of the Plowden recommendations have been widely adopted. A survey of 114 primary schools in Nottinghamshire (1978) found that 88 per cent had open evenings, and 85 per cent issued standing invitations to parents to visit the school and discuss their children's work (Bassey, 1978). However, there is less evidence of thorough-going attempts to explain schools' organizations and teaching methods. Primary schools may publish prospectuses, but they rarely give detailed accounts of the work of the schools—such as the names of the reading and mathematics schemes used, or the methods of grouping children within classes. The Newsons, after interviewing the mothers of 700 seven year olds in Nottingham (1977) commented: 'We found almost no instance of a school going out of its way to introduce parents to the means by which the teaching of reading was approached in order to enlist their informed help.' As Jackson and Marsden pointed out, teachers face a stupendous task if they want working class parents to have a real understanding of the educational system and its methods; the practices at present employed seem to be still inadequate.

2   Increasing access to school and staff

This is a widely adopted form of parent involvement. Few schools nowadays ward off parents with a notice that TRESPASSERS WILL BE PROSECUTED. It is normal practice in nursery schools to invite parents to spend time in class if they wish, and parents' rooms, coffee mornings, and social evenings are frequently organized. The Nottinghamshire survey of primary schools found that 58 per cent have an 'open house', that is that parents are welcome to visit the school at any time to see their children at work, and 59 per cent have special open days for this purpose.

3 Inviting parents' help in a non-teaching capacity

This is also a widespread form of parent involvement, acceptable to a large number of teachers. Joyce Watt in a study of all the 39 nursery schools and classes in Fife, Scotland (1977) found that two thirds invited parents to accompany them on school outings. The Nottinghamshire primary school survey found that in 82 per cent of schools parents helped on school outings, and in 75 per cent they accompanied swimming parties.

4 Inviting parents' help in a teaching capacity

The Nottinghamshire primary inspectors' report stated that parents helped teachers in nearly a third of the seven year old classes. In over two thirds of the classes where help was given parents were involved with children's learning, usually in hearing children read. The survey revealed that 54 per cent of the schools had parents help with reading, 56 per cent with cooking, and 65 per cent with needlework. The proportion of parents involved was probably small. In a typical week, two thirds of the schools had ten or fewer parents giving voluntary help of any kind, while the pupils numbered several hundred. It must be much rarer for parents to be asked to contribute their particular skills and knowledge, rather than help with routine class activities. In the survey referred to, the Newsons stated: 'We did not have one example of the father's or the mother's work experience being deliberately made use of by the school.'

5 Reaching into the community

Midwinter's innovatory schemes for 'selling' the school to the community do not seem to have been taken up elsewhere. Some authorities have appointed a few home-school liaison teachers, or home visitors, a very small number of community primary schools have been set up, which organize out-of-school activities with parents and provide community facilities, and a much larger but unknown number of primary schools provide book and toy libraries for their children. Joyce Watt's survey showed that a third of nursery schools did some home visiting, but the proportion of parents visited is not known. The high cost of most parent involvement activities that fall under this heading has probably limited their spread.

6 Consulting parents or involving them in management

The appointment of one or two parent governors is now general practice, but there is little evidence that many teachers consider it profitable to consult the parents with whom they work, or turn to them for information, opinions or suggestions.

Opposition to parent involvement

While some forms of parent involvement have been adopted quite widely, others usually evoke outright opposition from teachers. This is especially the case with asking parents to help in the classroom in a teaching capacity, and involving them in any way in decision-making. Both these practices constitute an encroachment by parents on the teachers' role: the issues raised are discussed further in Chapter 7.

Joan Tough, for example, whose Schools Council project *Communication skills in early childhood* (1971–6) provided in-service training for thousands of nursery and infant teachers, advises caution about bringing parents in the classroom. 'If we can increase the mother's knowledge of school, and help her to be interested in her own child's development, we will be justified in bringing her in to help on a regular basis. But bringing unpaid, untrained help into schools has its problems, and we would not want to give children experiences that were not appropriate and valuable' (1977).

Behind this caution there is a strong sense that education is a matter to be left to professionals. This is also, of course, the argument of the National Union of Teachers. In their policy document *Parents in Schools* (1979), the arguments for involving parents in school raised by Plowden, Bullock, the EPA Project, ACE, CASE, and the playgroup movement are neither stated nor countered. It is conceded that parents can fruitfully give practical help by acting as escorts on journeys, repairing books, and so on. However, grave reservations are expressed about involving them in activities which call for the exercise of professional educative skills. The practice of asking parents to hear children read in school is particularly deprecated. Not only are parents said to lack the necessary expertise for this, but the practice is claimed to raise issues of professional confidentiality, insurance coverage, and legal responsibility. However, despite this opposition, government publications (such as the White Paper of 1972, *Education: a Framework for Expansion*) continue to see parental involvement in nursery and infant classrooms as an important educational measure.

Is parent involvement effective?

Even today, educational innovations in Britain tend to be made without any attempt to evaluate whether they have achieved their goals, and parent involvement is no exception. Official advocacy of parent involvement is based on the belief that it will raise educational levels. If the Plowden and Bullock recommendations achieved this end, parent involvement would certainly be a cheap and effective educational instrument.

Unfortunately, there is little evidence that activities such as open evenings, inviting parents into the classroom, and starting mothers' clubs lead to significant educational advance. In Britain very few studies of the question have been made.

Parent involvement has generally been one part of a larger educational package, as in the EPA project, so that its effects could not be isolated. In other cases the research has been carried out without adequate controls (cf. Young and McGeeney, 1968).

The evidence that does exist, both from this country and from the much greater volume of research in the USA, suggests that something very different from the usual parent involvement programme is needed to raise achievement or IQ levels.

Educational objectives need to be specific, rather than general; methods need to be geared to these objectives and regular individual contact with all parents, either in the school or in their homes, is required. (See the studies cited on pages 27–8 and the discussion in Bronfenbrenner, 1974.) These methods will not, it should be noted, equalize educational achievement between social classes—middle class children whose parents are involved or who hear about the methods will make as large a gain as working class parents, thus maintaining the social class gap.

Further, unless work with individual parents continues from the preschool into the primary school, the children's educational levels will not be raised. It must be said, though, that some recent American studies of the long-term effects of preschool Head Start programmes have suggested that this latter view is unduly pessimistic. Even though the children's educational levels were not raised in the first years at school, their progress eight years or so later did appear to be affected (Lazar *et al.*, 1977). This long-term effect was mainly on the proportion of very backward children in the group. Fewer ex-Head Start pupils than controls were found in special classes for the retarded or had been made to repeat a year in class.

Caution is needed in generalizing from these findings. The Head Start children came from more deprived backgrounds than those in any comparable British study and the average IQ of most of the groups at follow-up was below 85. Further, the preschools they had attended were very unlike British nursery schools, with a much higher adult-child ratio, a curriculum focused on cognitive objectives, and the involvement of parents in teaching their children. It is certainly not as yet legitimate to infer that attendance at a British nursery school, with or without the British style of parent involvement, will have long-term effects on the educational achievements of ordinary working class children in this country. But there *is* evidence that organized, systematic work with individual parents will improve the current levels of childrens' attainments.

It does not, of course, follow that parent involvement activities which do not increase children's achievements are of no value. There are other aims of parent involvement, discussed in the first chapter. Some of these do not require evaluation—for instance, the assertion that parents have a right to information and consultation. Others, such as the claim that parents and children benefit emotionally from closer home-school links, or that parents' and children's attitudes to school become more positive if their parents are involved, could well be investigated.

Most attempts to discover whether a particular parent involvement activity had achieved the aim for which it was intended would require feedback from the parents concerned. But throughout the debate on parent involvement singularly few attempts seem to have been made to seek the views of parents, or even to describe their reactions to the attempts to involve them. We don't know, for example, in what circumstances mothers feel enriched by helping in playgroups and nursery schools, or in what circumstances the reverse is true, and parent participation is experienced as a new and extra burden.*

This issue is not an academic one: without attempts to see whether innovations achieve their aims, they may well misfire. In the course of the research project which is described in this

* After this book was finished Teresa Smith's account of parent involvement in Oxfordshire nursery classes and playgroups, *Parents and Preschool* (1980) was published. In this project parents were interviewed about the extent of their involvement in preschool, and their views on a variety of parent activities.

book we tried to make good these omissions. As the reader will see, our attempts were not entirely successful, but we hope that they will serve to advance the discussion further.

3

Parent involvement in action

Attitudes at the start of the project

We have already pointed out that there is a discrepancy between the approval of the *principle* of parent involvement in early education and the extent to which it is realized in practice. There also seems to be a discrepancy between the desire expressed by some teachers to involve parents in their children's schools, and the extent to which parents, especially in disadvantaged areas, respond to their invitations. Although opinions abound on the reasons for these discrepancies no systematic study of them has been undertaken. Yet without a greater understanding of the factors underlying the success or failure of a school's attempts to involve parents, further progress is likely to be slow.

It seemed to us important to discover why some parents did take up opportunities for parent involvement, and others did not. We also wanted to find out what kind of involvement parents preferred. Did they want to be consulted by the teachers, or to take part in decision-making, or were they principally interested in receiving more information about their child's education? Did parents find it satisfying to help in the classroom, and if not, what did they dislike about it?

The factors underlying teachers' attitudes to parent involvement also need study. Do even those teachers who introduce methods of involving parents have mixed feelings about the innovations? If so, what are the reasons for this? For example, does their uneasiness stem from anxiety about maintaining their own status, from the extra burdens or the conflict of roles which this work puts on them, or from the difficulties of communicating with parents who might not share their attitudes and values?

We decided to attempt to answer these questions by studying what happened when extra resources were supplied for parent involvement programmes in nursery schools and classes. We opted to work intensively in a small number of schools—just seven—situated in very different areas, to allow each teacher to work out her own parent involvement programme, and to modify it in the course of the project if this would help to clarify the issue. The project was therefore less an experiment than a descriptive study of parent involvement in action, organized to explore the questions outlined above. The methods we used were as objective as we could make them—systematic observations, careful records, and prepared interviews given to all parents and teachers.

A second aim of the project was to develop detailed effective methods for working with parents. We found that many teachers, even when willing, were uncertain how to organize effective parent involvement—in their training they had often received little practical guidance in this area. In the second part of this book we describe a variety of ways in which specific aims can be transmitted into school practice, and evaluated by the teacher.

Overall strategy

The research team consisted of the director, Barbara Tizard, and three research officers, who were not only graduates but also experienced and competent teachers. For the first two years we helped the schools to develop and carry through parent involvement programmes. Staff and parents were interviewed at the start of the project, and at the end of the first and second years. We then withdrew from the schools, and had no further contact with them for a year. At the end of the third year we re-interviewed the staff and a sample of parents from all seven schools, to establish what remained of the programmes that had been set up, and how staff and parents now viewed parent involvement.

Selection of schools

It was not part of our project to convince teachers that they *should* involve parents—we wanted instead to study what happened when interested teachers introduced a parent involvement programme. We began, therefore, by looking for schools in a variety of social settings, where both the head and class teacher wanted to increase parent involvement, and to take part in our research. We finally selected our seven units, all in the London area, or within reach of London.

Unit A served a largely white, manual working class district in an industrial town. It was one class of a large nursery school, on a between-wars council estate. This unit was unusual in that it contained a large proportion of children from families who were designated social priority—that is, single parent or very large families. Only 16 per cent of the mothers were employed.

Unit B also served a white manual working class area, but had fewer children from 'social priority' families. It was a nursery class attached to a primary school in a large industrial city. Most of the families lived in small Victorian terraced houses. Twenty-one per cent of the mothers worked part-time.

Unit C was a nursery class near the centre of a large industrial town. It served rather more prosperous families than Units A and B; half of the fathers had white collar jobs. All the families were white. A third of the mothers were employed, mostly part-time.

Unit D was a nursery class in a spacious suburb. The families' housing ranged from expensive detached houses to Council flats. Most of the fathers were white collar workers, and many were in professional occupations. A quarter of the mothers worked, mostly part-time. Most families were white.

Unit E was one class in a large nursery school within the London area. At the start of the project 35 per cent of the families were Asian, 8 per cent West Indian, and the rest were white. The proportion of Asian and West Indian families increased during the project. The social class composition was very mixed, and the families housing ranged from owner-occupied semi-detached houses to council flats. More than a third of the mothers were employed.

Unit F was a small nursery school in the London area. 85 per cent of the families were Asian, mainly Sikhs, one family was West Indian, and the rest were English. Only 15 per cent of the fathers had white collar jobs, and most families lived in poor quality housing. Some of the parents were highly educated East African Asians, who were nevertheless working in unskilled manual jobs. Others came from villages in the Punjab and the mothers, in particular, had received little education. All the teachers were British and white; there was a Punjabi-speaking East African assistant. Nearly half the mothers worked, often full-time.

Unit G was a nursery in a working class multi-racial area of London. Half the families were English or Irish. Most of the others came from the West Indies and Cyprus, and a few from

India, Mauritius and Africa. Most families lived in small privately owned or rented terraced houses or flats. The nursery teacher and assistant were both British and white. Over half of the mothers worked, often full-time.

The seven units thus differed considerably in the social class composition and educational level of their families. The units with a large proportion of non-indigenous children differed from the rest in three respects, each highly relevant to the question of parent involvement. These were that, in addition to cultural differences between staff and parents, there was often an absence of a common language; and also that a substantial proportion of mothers worked, many full-time. Their children were almost always cared for out of school hours by relatives— grandparents, parents working complementary shifts, or even brothers and sisters.

The nursery units

All the nursery units cared for three and four year olds, in mixed age groups of 24–33 children. They were staffed by trained teachers and assistants, with a staff-child ratio varying between 1:10 and 1:14. They were run largely on 'free-play' lines, but some units introduced four year olds to writing, some tried to see all the children did certain activities each day (such as a craft activity) while others left the children almost entirely to choose their own activities.

Home-school contacts at the outset of the study

In all the nursery units the mother was asked to stay with her child for a varying period of time when he first started school, to 'settle' him. Three teachers already had an active parent in- volvement programme which they wanted to expand; for instance one of them had a rota of parents to help in the class, ran a regular discussion group for mothers, and arranged a 15-minute discussion about each child twice yearly with his parents. Predictably, these were the most middle class units—that is, the schools where the parents had received the most education, and where the proportion of fathers in white collar jobs was largest. In the other four units the teachers relied mainly on informal day-to-day contacts with parents—several had tried to hold evening meetings but had given them up because of poor attendance; most invited mothers to help in the class, but few mothers took up the invitation.

Since all the teachers laid stress on their daily contacts with parents, we decided to start by observing parent-staff conversations over a five day period. The number of conversations varied widely; in one school 96 per cent of parents had at least one conversation per day with the staff, in another 20 per cent of the parents had no conversations at all with the staff during the five days. Most of this variation stemmed from differences in the classroom routine. In some units the teacher deliberately freed herself at the beginning and end of the session to talk to parents, while in others she was occupied at these times, setting out or clearing up equipment or organizing a music or story session.

The majority of the conversations consisted of greetings and comments on the weather. The other major group of topics concerned the children's health, school milk, and school meals. There was little or no evidence of the teachers' attempting to give detailed information or suggestions to parents, telling them for instance what the child had been learning that morning, or suggesting how this might be followed up at home, and no evidence of them consulting the parents or seeking their opinions. A mother's queries were almost always general questions about whether her child had been good or happy, which were met with equally general responses, supplemented perhaps with the comment that he had done a nice painting. The child's home activities were hardly ever discussed.

Of course, parents are often in a hurry when they bring and

collect their children, and staff may be preoccupied with other duties. It may therefore be unrealistic to expect much more than a friendly exchange of greetings at these times. We often found, however, that staff believed such conversations *did* serve a vital purpose. In discussion with teachers we were frequently told that formal structures for parent-teacher contact, such as home visits or individual appointments, were unnecessary in the nursery school, because of the frequent informal contacts that already occurred. Yet in the course of our project we found that these informal contacts very rarely gave rise to any but the briefest chat. It seems likely that even when teacher and parent meet twice a day, formal arrangements *are* needed to ensure that every parent has an opportunity to discuss her child.

Staff and parent views on the aims of nursery education

After the observations were completed we interviewed the heads and class teachers in the schools, and the mothers in their homes, where necessary with an interpreter. Most advocates of parent involvement, from whatever point of view, have stressed that at the heart of the matter is the need for parents to understand what the school is doing and why. We therefore started by asking both parents and staff what they saw as the aims of nursery education.

The most frequent answer, given by 11 of our 14 staff,* was that they hoped to further the children's intellectual development by stimulating, or 'stretching' them, or by enriching their language, usually through the medium of play. Five staff saw this aim in relation to the deficiencies of the children's homes— 'to provide the children with what they don't get at home—toys, talk, explanations'; 'to give them what a really good home would provide, stimulation and a rich environment'.

* Since there were no obvious systematic differences between the answers given during the interviews by heads and class teachers we have reported them together.

Six staff said that in addition they aimed to give the children security, 'mothering' or happiness, and four of them saw this as compensating for the hardships of the children's lives. 'These kids are going to have problems all their lives. How can they know how to live if they've never been happy? So we try to give them two and a half hours of happiness.' 'For some of our children the most important thing we can give is security.' Four staff said that they wanted to help children learn to mix with other children, and to adapt to a school environment.

None of the staff mentioned as one of their aims teaching English as a second language. Yet all of them had at least one child from a family where English was either not spoken at home, or was not the first language, and three teachers had a substantial proportion of such children. This does not, of course, mean that they made no efforts to develop the children's English, but that they did not see this as a priority at the nursery stage.

Most of the mothers appeared unaware that the teachers were concerned with the children's intellectual development. They saw the nursery as a place where children learned to mix together, learned rhymes and songs, drawing and painting, and in the case of Asian children, English. A substantial minority were critical of this curriculum, and thought that their children were 'just playing about at school'. Between a half and a fifth of parents in all the units would have liked the children to start on reading and writing; others mentioned swimming and music. But few parents had expressed these views to the teachers. They explained their diffidence by saying that 'the teacher must know best', or 'the teacher is too busy'. Other mothers said that they didn't want to seem 'pushy' or get a reputation for being 'awkward'.

Despite their reservations, at least 70 per cent of parents in all but one school—more in the middle class schools—said that they had no serious worries or dislikes about the school. Further, all but one or two parents in each school said that their children usually enjoyed going to school.

45

The staff's perception of the parents' attitudes to their schools was fairly accurate. Eleven of the 14 staff thought that the parents appreciated the school: 'Definitely. I have only to ask, and I get all the help I need.' 'The longer he's here the more they appreciate it.' However, most were aware that a proportion of parents were critical of the nursery methods. 'I would like the parents to be more interested in what the children do here and what they learn through play. What the *parents* would like is for us to teach them to count—like so many parrots.' In fact, in only two of the seven schools (the most middle class in the project) did the staff feel that the majority of the parents *understood* what the school was trying to do. The more common view was that 'they may have a vague idea. But most of them think that when he starts infant school, that's when it's important.'

Views of the parents' educational role

Not only did the parents tend to view the nursery school differently from the staff, they also saw their own educational role differently. The staff considered that parents could best help their children by playing with them, reading to them and developing their language. But except in the middle class units they doubted whether many parents did in fact help in these ways, and six of the 14 staff thought that the parents made *no* positive contribution to their children's education at all. 'Well, parents ought to make a contribution, but our parents lack education.' The same six staff could not name anything which children learnt better at home than at school. Typical comments were: 'In an enabling middle class home, yes, but not round here.' 'To be frank, the children are better off in school.'

Of course, this did not mean that the staff felt the parents gave nothing of value to the children. Most of them stressed the parents' concern and affection for the children, and the role they played in their children's social and emotional development. 'There's a lot of basically good mothering, and a lot of concern for the children.' 'Asian families are very affectionate, caring and peaceful. They're relaxed with their children, never agitated.' But nearly half of the staff interviewed, especially those in units serving non-indigenous families, were critical of the parents as educators. Some attributed what they saw as deficiencies to the parents' social problems. 'There are just too many stresses on our families—both parents working, poor housing, too many children. They have no time to spare; and they're often worn out.' These teachers implicitly assumed that if the parents were less stressed they would read more often to their children, put them to bed earlier, and so on. Other teachers considered that as well as having social problems, the parents simply did not know what was best for their children.

It was certainly the case that most of the mothers we interviewed did not share the staff's view of their educational role. In all except the most middle class unit, D, they tended to see their own major teaching role in terms of instilling discipline, manners, and values. In so far as they defined a role for themselves in the children's *intellectual* development, it was largely to help them with the 'three Rs'. In every school between two fifths and three quarters of parents were, unbeknown to the staff, trying to teach their children to write, count, and in some cases also to read. This does not, of course, mean that they *were not* helping their children's intellectual development in a variety of ways, but they were generally not conscious of doing so, and did not see reading aloud and playing with their child as 'educational activities'.

Staff attitude to parent involvement

We asked the staff what, in their opinion, might stand in the way of increasing parent involvement. The obstacle most frequently mentioned was the parents' unwillingness: 'The main obstacle is the parents. They may be shy, or afraid of the school, or have to work, or they don't speak English, but anyway they don't come.'

A minority suggested that the obstacles might be created by the teacher: 'Teachers may be reserved, they may feel they can't cope with parents.' Or by social class differences: 'To be frank it's not easy to get through to people of quite a different social class.' Three teachers mentioned problems of space, building design, or the limited time available to teachers.

The staff in the two schools with a large proportion of Asian parents were in addition very aware of cultural and language barriers. 'We don't understand the Asian parents very well. They're generous when you get to know them, but extremely sensitive about the way in which they're treated. We need an Asian teacher and an Asian social worker to help us.'

All but two of the staff saw potential dangers in trying to increase parent involvement. Some were concerned about their authority. 'You must be firm. Otherwise, if you give them half a chance, they'd take over the place.' Others stressed the difficulty of competing demands on their time. 'I feel torn between the parents and the children. I feel I should give more time to the parents, but if I didn't work with the children, the assistants wouldn't. It's very hard to know how to distribute my attention.' One teacher frankly said 'I'd be put on the spot. Parent involvement needs someone confident and ready to take on anything, and I'm not sure how well I would manage.' Two teachers saw *no* potential dangers. 'Dangers or problems?—no. There are built-in safeguards for the teacher in the system.'

Staff reasons for wanting an increase in parent involvement

One teacher was interested in parent involvement simply because she thought children would benefit from a close liaison between staff and parents. But most of the staff had other reasons. They wanted to influence child rearing practices: 'The time at home could be much more beneficially spent. If only parents understood what we are trying to do it could be "nursery" all day.' They also wanted to have the satisfaction of feeling that their own work was not only appreciated, but also understood by the parents. The issue of the parents' right to be informed or consulted about their children's education was not raised by any staff, and they did not, like many playgroup leaders, see parent involvement as a way of enriching mothers' lives. The staff in the two schools where a large proportion of the parents were Asian felt they should incorporate aspects of Asian culture into the school, and in these schools we worked closely with the community education team.* In the other schools parent involvement was not seen as a way in which the parents and the community could make a contribution to the school, nor did most of the staff feel a need to consult the parents about their children.

These attitudes were in line with current main stream educational thinking, as documented in the Bullock Report. Both in the meaning they gave to the term 'parental involvement', and the reasons for which they advocated it, the teachers in our project were probably representative of their profession. More than that, they were unusually committed—they had volunteered not only to join the project, but to put up with a research worker in the classroom as well.

Contradictions in staff attitudes

Yet there were certain contradictions in their position. Despite their wish to influence parents, most of them made little direct attempt to do so. At the outset of the project one teacher made home visits, and another had organized a discussion group for mothers about behaviour problems. For the most part their contacts with the parents were concerned with the child in

* Community education teams operate in a number of multi-cultural areas. They are most often concerned with home-school and community-school liaison, and with organizing English language teaching for parents and children.

school, and not with his out-of-school activities. This was no doubt because involvement in the children's home lives had not featured in their training, nor was it part of their role definition. Further, some staff, while anxious to influence parents, felt that many had too many pressures on them already, and that they should not be burdened with further pressures from the school. Most thought that the best way to influence parents would be to attract them into school. 'If they see the value of what we're doing they might go and do it themselves.'

At the same time, all the staff were conscious of difficulties, even dangers, in this particular course of action. These were in part organizational—the fragmentation of the teacher's time and attention when parents are in the classroom was frequently mentioned—and in part concerned with possible threats to her authority. Our interviews with the parents suggested that this was not very real. Most parents were reluctant even to make suggestions to the staff, both because of their feelings that the teacher must know best, and because of their anxiety not to provoke her displeasure.

This chapter describes the state of play, as far as staff and parent attitudes were concerned, at the start of the project. The changes that occurred in the course of the project are recorded in the next chapter.

4

Two years of intervention

Our strategy in working with the teachers was to discuss with each one of them our observations of the current state of parent-teacher contacts in their classes, and the attitudes of the parents as expressed to us in interviews. We then went on to work out with them their aims for a parent involvement programme, and appropriate methods to achieve these aims.

It was generally the case that the staff implicitly held a 'one-way' model of parent involvement—they wished to change some aspects of the parents' behaviour in order, as they believed, to benefit the children educationally. They did not see a need for school practice to change in response to input from the parents. The research team thought it important to start by accepting this viewpoint, but also to discuss from time to time the merits of a two-way model, either in general terms, or more often in relation to a specific activity. For example, if a class library was to be set up, we might suggest that parents could be involved in the choice of books and the decision about opening times, and could help to monitor and evaluate the running of the library.

The teachers were, of course, quite free to reject these suggestions; in each case we worked out with them a parent involvement programme which they found acceptable. We then provided additional resources—mainly equipment, such as video-cameras, and an extra pair of hands—to help carry out and evaluate the success of the activities.

The research officers spent two days a week in each school for the first year. Because of staff problems, in the second year of the project we were only able to make occasional visits to four of the seven schools. In addition, we held twice-termly meetings in London which were attended regularly by the seven class teachers, most of the heads, and some nursery assistants and primary advisors.

Each of the teachers organized a rather different programme of activities; what they chose to do depended on their attitudes and priorities, and the physical limitations of the building. For example, some teachers responded to our observations of their contacts with parents by reorganizing their classroom routines, so that they were more available to parents at arrival and departure times. Others took no action, or decided it would be preferable to make definite appointments to see all the mothers. Some teachers responded to the parents' interest in reading and writing by organizing 'writing workshops' for parents, and discussing home reading schemes with them, and some decided to teach the older children to write at school, while others on the other hand ignored or tried to discourage the parents' interest in reading and writing. Some classrooms had space for a 'parents' area', and even for a small group of toddlers to spend the morning in one part of the room with their mothers. Other classrooms, though, could not comfortably have housed more than a few extra adults.

At the end of the first year we re-interviewed staff and parents, and the second year's activities were planned with the teachers in light of these findings. Questionnaires were issued to the parents at the end of the second year of intervention.

Activities organized during the two years by one school or another are listed below under the aim which they were intended to fulfil; a more detailed description of their organization is given in the second half of the book. Some of the aims (such as communicating the teachers' aims and methods, widening parents' educational horizons) were those initially put forward by the teachers. Others (like involving parents in helping their children at home, or organizing an exchange of views with parents) emerged during the course of the project, as a result of discussing the interview findings and of discussions between all the project teachers.

Communicating the teachers' aims and methods

The activities organized with this aim included the production of class prospectuses, fortnightly newsletters, and instant picture camera records of outings and activities displayed on a noticeboard. Coffee mornings were held for a few parents at a time, as well as class parents' evenings, at which play materials, films, video films and slide shows of the children in the nursery were shown and explained, or the relationship between nursery activities and the development of literacy and numeracy was discussed. Displays were set up in the nursery for parents unable to attend these meetings. One teacher, who started teaching reading and writing to four year olds, made a video recording of her teaching to show parents. Copies of rhymes and songs used at schools were sent home. 'Open sessions' were organized once a week, when parents could not only watch the children, but staff were free to discuss and explain their activities. Chalked notices were put on a blackboard by the door at the end of each session, to inform the parents about an activity which had been done that day, and how it was intended to help the children. A series of illustrated leaflets were produced by the research staff each of which explained the purpose of a particular play material, described the developmental sequences in the child's use of it, and suggested activities which could be carried out at home to foster similar processes; 'parents' areas' were organized in the classroom, with easy chairs, kettles, parents' noticeboards, etc. In one school a 'mother and toddler club' was started, primarily for the younger siblings of the nursery children, and for other two year olds on the waiting list. The club met once a week in the lunch hour, and was run by the teacher (who gave up her free time) and two parents. The teacher saw the club as an opportunity to discuss play, books, and nursery education with the mothers at an early stage; in addition, she hoped to ease the children's transition to the nursery class. In the predominantly 'Asian' school, the wall notices and letters sent home were written by bi-lingual mothers in the main language of the parents, and twice-weekly English classes for mothers were held in the lunch hour. The language teacher was provided by the local community education team, and the school staff, in their free time, kept an eye on the children of the mothers' involved.

Widening parents' educational horizons

Small groups of parents were taken to visit the children's public libraries, specialist toy shops, and holiday play centres. Lists of holiday outings and activities were prepared. Classroom book and toy libraries were organized, as well as exhibitions and sales of books and toys, and the local children's librarian talked to parents' meetings.

An interesting example of an abortive attempt in one school to widen parents' educational horizons was an 'infant school' project. This never took place, because it did not appeal to the local head teachers. The parents in this school, as in most others, were very interested in modern primary schools methods. Rather than lecture them, we planned to develop their interest by showing them the variations of practice that exist. We hoped to arrange an initial meeting about primary education, and then take parents in small groups to visit the local infant schools. At the final session we planned a discussion between the parents and nursery staff about what they had seen. The aim of the exercise was not to nominate a 'best buy' among the local infant schools (and in fact most of the parents had little choice about the school to which they would send their children). It was rather to give them concrete information about the range of practices in infant schools, and thus provide them with an informed basis for discussing primary education.

In the event, none of the infant heads concerned agreed to take part in this project. While they would have welcomed visits by individual parents, they disliked the idea of having their schools compared and discussed by groups of parents.

Involving parents in helping their children at home

'Writing workshops' were held for parents, to show them the best way to help their children write. 'Work folders' were sent home with examples of the children's creative products, and suggestions for activities for parents to try at home with their children. One teacher used these work folders with the older children to introduce them to reading and writing, and discussed the children's progress through them individually with the parents. Another teacher lent copies of a commercial home-teaching early reading scheme to several mothers, who used it at home, and discussed the children's progress with the teachers. 'Holiday kits' were prepared with activities for children to do at home—for instance mazes and puzzles. Commercial 'play-packs' were lent to mothers to use with their children at home, and the value or otherwise of the activities were discussed in a 'club' at school with the teacher and the other mothers.

Increasing parental contributions at school

In some schools parents made a big contribution to many of the activities already listed (helping to write newsletters, for example, or helping to select books and run the class library, preparing lists of holiday outings, or helping to run the mother and toddler club). In others, the staff were unwilling to delegate or share responsibility. Other contributions from parents included helping 'new' parents and children to settle-in; helping in the class by reading to, or playing with, children; taking a group for cooking; or introducing them to the parents' own interests—as by taking small groups to an allotment or going on mini-outings with children and staff. Asian mothers showed staff and children how to cook pilau and sweetmeats; they provided food, dancing and singing at Christmas and Jubilee parties, dressed dolls, brought in Punjabi clothes for dressing up, domestic equipment for the home corner, and Indian fruit and vegetables, cereal and spices for display. In one school, parents started a 'thrift club' to raise money for a classroom library; in another, one mother helped with three non-English speaking children. This mother and the teacher together visited a specialist in English as a second language to discuss suitable methods and materials. They then drew up a programme of work, and arranged that by their joint efforts each child should have at least half an hour's intensive language work a day. Often the volunteer mother took the children on mini-excursions to shops, or railway stations to help increase their vocabulary. In one school the class library became the focus for a 'library hour', in which parents read to the children, and discussed children's books with the staff (See pages 187–97); in another school mothers wrote and illustrated books for the class library (see pages 194–7).

Organizing an exchange of views with parents

In three of the seven schools parents' meetings were organized to elicit parents' views, rather than, as is more usual, to seek their help or give them the teachers' views or invite questions. In one school a number of such meetings were held in the mornings, in an empty classroom. The nursery assistant and a teacher-trained mother took over the class, and the mothers brought their toddlers and babies with them. Topics discussed included problems in the transition to infant school, possible parental contributions to the class, what kinds of extra equipment were most needed in the class, and how to raise funds for them, the pros and cons of parents helping in the classroom. One mother took notes of the discussion and circulated them to parents who couldn't come. In the other two schools only two meetings were held; one was concerned with the parents' reactions to the parent involvement programme. In the third school a discussion meeting centred around a video recording of dinner time in the infant school.

At an individual level, several of the teachers made home visits, and kept home-school diaries for parents who could not visit the school. One teacher made developmental assessments of the children, and discussed them with the parents, and another made twice-yearly appointments at school with each parent to discuss their child.

'Take-up' of activities by parents

Organizing activities by no means guarantees that parents will take part. Most projects which have involved parents, such as the EPA project, give very limited information about the proportion of parents involved, and the extent of their involvement. We kept detailed records of parental 'take-up': this varied greatly from school to school, but increased in all schools over the two year period.

Some interventions, such as giving out class prospectuses, called for nothing more active from the parents than to receive and perhaps read a piece of paper. Others, which we have called 'activities', involved a definite commitment of time and energy. In one school, for example, the parents could in one term have used the class library, attended an evening meeting, helped in the classroom, taken part in a parents' coffee morning, and helped to take children on an outing. Few parents took up all these invitations, but in the first year between 30 per cent and 68 per cent of mothers in each school had been involved in more than half of the activities arranged; in the second year the proportion varied between 50 per cent and 94 per cent.

Every mother had been involved in at least one activity, except in the multi-racial unit G, where nearly half were not involved at all during the first year, but only three mothers were not involved in the second year, and in the 'Asian' school, F, where several mothers were not involved at all. The proportion of fathers involved was a good deal smaller, and with the exception of two or three fathers in each class, their involvement was mainly confined to attending evening meetings.

The best patronized activities were the libraries, used by virtually all the parents in the indigenous schools, and the parents' meetings—between 66 per cent and 94 per cent of mothers attended at least one a year, and about half the fathers did so. Before the project, parents' meetings had been abandoned by several of the schools because of poor attendance. The high attendance during the project seems due to a number of factors—some schools repeated meetings, so that parents could attend either during the day or in the evening; some provided crèches; all meetings centred round topics of immediate interest to parents; and all were extensively publicized.

The proportion of mothers who had helped at least once in the nursery varied from 75 per cent in the most middle class unit, D, through 33 per cent in most of the others, to only one mother in the multi-racial unit, G. In most classes one or two fathers also helped. Forty per cent of the mothers in unit D helped regularly, on a rota basis, but this was true of only a few mothers in the other classes.

Our project demonstrated that given extra resources almost all mothers and about 50 per cent of fathers can be drawn into one aspect or another of a nursery parent involvement programme, provided that staff are prepared to visit some parents at home, and provided that when necessary a bilingual relative or friend is available to act as interpreter.

Parents' views of parent involvement activities

At the end of the second year, we issued a questionnaire about the activities which had been organized in each school. For each activity, we asked parents to tick any statements they agreed with in a list of favourable and unfavourable comments, and to add further comments if they wished. The proportion of parents who, after reminders, returned the questionnaire varied from 82 per cent in the most middle class school to only 20 per cent in the multi-racial school. For many parents, filling up researchers' questionnaires is a low priority occupation; interviewing parents in their homes is a much better, although expensive, way of eliciting their views. The comments reported below probably represent the views of the most interested parents; reservations and criticisms, therefore, are of particular interest.

Many favourable, and very few unfavourable comments, were made about most of the activities. There were two exceptions, helping in the class, and toy libraries, both of which received a substantial number of unfavourable complaints (see pages 71–80 and 175–87). The most frequently occurring complaint about helping in the class related to a feeling of uncertainty. 'I didn't know what to do when the children quarrelled.' 'I would have liked a definite job to do.' 'I didn't feel as if I was doing anything useful.' Most of the favourable comments referred to the mothers' pleasure in watching their own and other children in a school setting. In one school, where the teacher only called in parents when she was shorthanded, most comments were favourable, and these mothers made it clear that what they enjoyed was the responsibility. 'I had a feeling of achievement.' 'I enjoyed being treated as an equal by the staff.'

Parents' attitudes to the programme

In the questionnaire we asked parents whether they thought that enough had been done to involve them in their children's education. Despite the extensive programme of activities, nearly a half of the parents who answered said no. The three most frequent types of comment added centred on information about how children were getting on, how to help them at home, and what the teachers' methods were. 'Show us the teaching methods, so we can continue them at home,' was a typical comment.

Of those parents who answered yes, much the most frequent comment was that a very good job had already been done. In every class a few parents suggested that parent involvement had gone rather too far. 'Any more would be overpowering.' 'Personally, I seem to have been involved quite enough.'

In answer to a query about whether they would welcome more advice of any kind, the great majority of parents in all the units said that they would. The exceptions were 'Asian' unit, F, and unit A, which had the most 'social priority' families. The kind of advice most often sought concerned helping children with their education at home, but there was also a considerable demand for suggestions for holiday and weekend activities. Advice about behaviour problems and health was wanted much less often, many parents considering that the staff were not qualified to give it.

Special problems in non-indigenous schools

Although parental involvement in these three schools increased during the project, most activities were less well patronized than those in the indigenous schools, and some were an outright failure. (Parents' evenings were an exception, being very well attended when video recordings of the nursery class were shown.) Toy libraries set up in two of the schools were closed down by the staff because of loss and damage, and one book library was closed for the same reason. The situation in each school was different; in the 'Asian' units lack of a common language was a serious problem, and in all three units a third of the mothers worked full time.

The staff in these units often became discouraged. 'There's a general lack of understanding and interest. Sometimes I feel the parents totally lack interest, at other times I think they just haven't got the time.'

In the multi-racial school, G, because of the poor response of many of the parents to most of the activities offered, a research officer paid an extra visit to the mothers in their homes to try to get a better understanding of their attitudes to education. It became clear that despite their reluctance to visit the school, most of the mothers were very concerned about their children's education. Three quarters of the mothers visited were not born in the UK, and English was often not their first language. Despite this, most of these mothers made a point of speaking English to their children, even though their grasp of the language was not always adequate, in the belief that this would be of benefit. This issue had not been discussed between the parents and the school staff.

Almost all the mothers felt that it was very important that their children got good educational qualifications. Half named professional occupations they would like their children to enter—medicine, accountancy, teaching, for instance—and all said that they thought they had good chances of doing so. When we asked them (without offering any suggestions), if they could spend more money on their children, how they would spend it, the most frequent answer was that they would like to send their child to a private school, or to a private tutor.

This visit led to the 'book project', in which each of the mothers approached wrote and illustrated a book for the class library (see pages 194–7). It was certainly not the case that the parents were not interested in their children's education. Many factors probably contributed to their reluctance to spend time in the school, or to take up the facilities offered them. Half the mothers were working; two thirds had grown up in a very different culture, with a very different educational system. They viewed toys as a way to keep children amused, rather than as a way of helping them to develop. Books tended to be given to children to look at on their own, or used to teach the alphabet. The parents expected to leave the child at the school door to be taught by the teacher, and the notion of lingering in the classroom was very unfamiliar to them. They were also puzzled that the children were not taught to read and write.

With hindsight, it seemed to us that there were two very different approaches which might have engendered enthusiasm in this class. Many of the parents were very concerned that their children should learn good English. Yet the nursery teacher seemed relatively unconcerned about the linguistic background of the children, and paid neither more nor less attention to language teaching than if she had been teaching an indigenous class. If she had put more emphasis in her work on English as a second language, kept records of the children's progress, discussed them with the parents, and suggested ways in which the parents could best help the children to improve their English, she would probably have met with a warmer response.

An alternative (or additional) approach would have been to attempt to capitalize on the cultural diversity in the class, by encouraging the parents to contribute from their own culture in ways which might have led to the development of friendships between parents and a more positive attitude to the school. It is quite possible, for example, that the parents could have been involved in making costumes, preparing food and showing the school how to celebrate the carnivals or festivals which were important to their families. If these activities resulted in closer personal relationships the teacher might then have found it easier to discuss educational issues with the parents.

It is not likely, though, that parental contributions without such discussions would have solved the problem of differing staff and parent attitudes to education. In the 'Asian' schools, the parents *did* make a cultural contribution, but continued to find the nursery schools puzzling. The cultural differences between staff and parents were very great. For example, implicit in the teachers' approach to nursery education were the beliefs that a certain amount of dirtiness and disorder is desirable or at least acceptable in children; that imagination, creativity, and self-initiation are important goals; and that reading for pleasure is self-evidently desirable. But parents who put a high value on hard work, cleanliness, obedience, and the acquisition of skills will not warm to the sight of their children splashing in the water tray, or feel enthusiastic about his 'creations'—which look to them like scribbles, or daubs of paint. They would prefer to see him 'settling down concentrating', or producing a line of carefully traced writing. Parents who don't themselves read for pleasure, however much they value reading for other purposes (for instance as a key to higher education) are not likely to approach children's books in the same spirit as those who are book lovers.

For these reasons it seemed to us unlikely that a sari in the dressing-up corner or Indian sweets at milk time would make nursery education either comprehensible or acceptable to the Asian parents. If the parents' priorities are for the children to learn to speak good English, to read and write, and to sit still when told to do so, they may not be too concerned about whether the play materials provided are of Asian or English origin.

What had the programme achieved?

There seems little doubt that in the largely indigenous schools most parents not only took part in the activities, but appreciated the teachers' efforts, and were aware that unusual opportunities were being offered them. This created an atmosphere of enthusiasm which went beyond the usual friendly staff-parent relationships. In the interviews and questionnaires many complimentary remarks were made about the teachers. Few parents appeared to have felt under pressure, and a frequent comment was that the teachers had done a splendid job. Awareness of the parents' appreciative responses was probably an important factor in the teachers' decision to continue parent involvement activities after the project had ended (see page 81), and was in itself for some teachers an adequate justification for the programme.

As we have seen the situation was not so rosy in the schools with a large proportion of non-indigenous families. There, fewer parents had been involved, some activities had been outright failures, and the parents seemed less appreciative of the teachers' efforts.

But increasing parental appreciation of staff had not been one of the original aims of the programme. Almost all the teachers had hoped to increase the parents' understanding of nursery education. By the end of the second year, in all the largely indigenous schools, between 75 per cent and 95 per cent of the mothers said that they understood and could explain the teacher's aims. In the most middle class school, D, the explanations offered were not unlike the teacher's, but in the other schools only a minority, sometimes a very small minority, mentioned general developmental aims such as intellectual or language development, or learning through play; the most frequent explanation given was that the teacher was preparing the children for infant school or teaching painting and stories. In the largely non-indigenous schools, only half the parents said that they understood the teacher's aims.

Preparation for infant school might be considered a reasonable shorthand summary of the purpose of nursery education, but when we probed further and asked why specific play materials are provided, the gap between teachers' and parents' understanding became apparent. The teachers' reasons, apart from giving the children enjoyment, were as follows: *sand and water*: to develop ideas of volume, properties of materials, and to develop language; *paint*: to develop creativity, and self-expression, to encourage the exploration of colour, shapes, etc.; *jig-saw puzzles*: to develop hand-eye coordination, and fine motor skills, to develop colour and shape discrimination; *home corner*: to stimulate cooperative play, to develop language, and to stimulate the imagination; *books*: to extend language and to stimulate the imagination.

After one year of the programme, 75 per cent of the mothers in the most middle class unit, D, gave reasonably similar answers, but hardly any mothers in the other units did so. The teachers would have been satisfied if the mothers had simply been aware that the children could learn *something* from the use of the materials, but in only two units, C and D, were four of the six play materials seen as 'for learning' by at least two thirds of the mothers. In the other schools, only one or two materials were described in these terms by two thirds of the mothers, and none at all in the 'Asian' unit, F. The material most often said to be 'for learning' was jigsaw puzzles, which were identified as such by at least two thirds of the mothers in all but the 'Asian' school. Sand and water, on the other hand, were least often seen as 'for learning'.

A number of mothers offered explanations for the provision of play materials which were far removed from those of the teachers. They illuminate the gap between the teachers and the mothers, and reveal how people, unfamiliar with the principles of nursery education, try to make sense of what they see. Thus the provision of water was explained as 'to get them interested in washing-up'; sand, 'to remind them of the seaside'; paint, 'to teach them how to draw faces properly'; puzzles, 'it's to test their IQ'. The most misunderstood piece of equipment was the home corner or wendy house. The teachers' aim in providing these miniature homes was to stimulate group imaginative play. Between 30 per cent and 50 per cent of parents in all the schools except D thought that they were intended either to provide early domestic science training 'it's to teach them to set the table' or 'it's to make it easier for them at school by reminding them what home is like'.

Except in units C and D, at the end of the first year most parents either didn't know why the materials were provided— 'It's never entered my head to ask'—or thought they were intended to keep the children happy or occupied. Critical comments about sand and water were common—'I don't know, and I don't like it, it's dangerous,' (sand); 'I don't know—so they'll get soaked through, I suppose,' (water). Between a third and a half of the Asian mothers did not know why any of the play materials were provided.

Despite the provision of class libraries, only about a half of mothers in four units gave answers which suggested that books were provided to increase the children's vocabulary or develop their imagination or general knowledge. Between 30 per cent and 60 per cent of mothers either said that they didn't know why books were provided—'I don't really know, they say he's too young to read,' or gave 'alternative' answers which suggested that they saw them primarily as reading primers—'to learn to recognize letters'—'they gradually learn to read from them'.

By the end of the second year, three quarters or more of the parents in the indigenous schools said that the play materials were 'for learning', although except in unit D few could explain what the child was supposed to be learning when he used them. Many parents in the non-indigenous schools remained mystified.

Our evidence suggests that unless efforts are specifically directed to explaining what the teacher sees to be the purpose of play materials, most mothers will think the activities are to keep the children amused. Visiting or helping in the classroom will not in itself bring parents closer to the teachers' point of view. What the mothers saw was children filling bottles of water: what the teachers saw was the children acquiring the foundations of science.

Even when the teachers tried to give specific explanations, the success of their efforts seemed to depend on the educational level and cultural background of the parents. In the indigenous schools they had considerable success in conveying the general notion that children learn through play. In the non-indigenous schools, their efforts were hampered by lack of a shared language, a great proportion of mothers unavailable because of full time work, and a different cultural tradition (see page 102).

The influence of the schools on the parents at home

Most of the teachers hoped that by seeing what went on in school the parents would act differently when their children were at home. At the end of both the first and second years we asked the mothers whether this had been the case. In the indigenous schools about half the mothers, on both occasions, said that they *had* been influenced: the most frequent example given was that they now allowed the children to play with water or other 'messy' materials, or had bought toys seen in the nursery. In the largely non-indigenous schools far fewer mothers said they had been influenced, either because they had not visited the school, or because 'things are not the same at home'. There was little evidence that the parents played more *with* the children, as the teachers had hoped—not surprisingly, perhaps since they were unlikely to see the *teachers* playing with the children (see page 101).

It was also the case that the provision of class libraries had not necessarily had the effects intended by the teachers. The proportion of mothers who said that they read to their children most days had slightly increased, but not all had acquired what might be called middle class reading habits. Children are most likely to be read to if there is a regular reading time, for instance, at bedtime, but less than half the mothers in most schools, and only a quarter of the mothers in the non-indigenous schools, had such a time. Half or fewer of the mothers in the non-indigenous schools read through a story—instead, they tended to talk about the pictures with their children, or use books as reading primers. Consequently they tended to choose books with large pictures and little text. The expensive, beautifully illustrated story books that appealed to the teachers were spurned by many mothers, who preferred to borrow Ladybird books and factual books. However, in the two units which, as well as providing a library, devoted much attention to involving parents in discussing children's books, and persuading them to read in school with their children, there was a substantial increase in 'reading through a book'.

Two-way discussion

The aim of increasing two-way discussion between teachers and parents proved difficult to implement. Three units held group discussions with parents about school practices, but in only one did lively debates develop. Even here mothers did not raise issues which they had brought up with us when we interviewed them at home. A number wanted their children to be taught to read, for instance, and others wanted to be shown how to further their children's education at home.

It seems likely that several reasons contributed to the parents' reluctance to express their views. In some of the schools the staff were not disposed to discuss educational issues with the parents, who were probably aware of their reluctance. Further, one result of the project was to increase the parents' respect for the teachers' professional skills. While initially the majority of parents had seen the nursery as a place where the children 'played about', the project information campaign persuaded many of them that this play was in fact 'educational'. The exposure of the parents to the teacher's terms—such as 'matching skills', 'hand-eye coordination', 'conservation of number'—served not only to raise her status but to inhibit criticism. It became more difficult for a parent to argue that her child should learn to read when she was told that first the child must play matching games to improve visual discrimination. It was not that the parent was necessarily convinced by this assertion, but rather that great confidence is required to pursue an argument with a professional if one is not conversant with the terms used.

The parents' appreciation of the parent involvement programme probably also served to diminish criticism. They were grateful for the efforts made by the staff, and correspondingly less disposed to complain. 'You can't criticize her, when she's doing so much,' was a comment made by several parents about a project teacher. An 'open' policy is probably an excellent way, whether intentional or not, to forestall parental criticisms; it seems possible, for example, that if the William Tyndale school staff had taken parents into their confidence at an early stage the crisis within the school might never have arisen.

Finally, some of the teachers did in fact respond to the parents' wishes without any open discussion between them— for instance they began to teach the older children to write. For all these reasons, as well as a fear of antagonizing the staff, even the middle class parents were reluctant to come forward with opinions and criticisms.

Although many parents helped in the class, only a minority of teachers used this opportunity to draw on their range of knowledge and skills—their musical or gardening talents, for example. Activities were usually initiated and closely directed by the staff, and parents were usually asked to help with the standard nursery activities.

Our attempts to devise ways in which teachers could show parents how to help their children at home also met with limited success. The teachers wanted to do this by encouraging parents to read and play with their children. But what the parents in all the schools wanted was to be shown how to help their children with their education, and it was clear that despite the teachers' campaign to explain nursery activities most parents except in the 'professional' school, D, did not see reading to and playing with their child as relevant to his future success at school. Those teachers who were prepared to show parents how to help their four year olds to start to read and write met with an enthusiastic response. But most of the project teachers were not prepared to do this, or would not have had the support of their heads and advisors in doing so.

Other ways in which we suggested parents might be encouraged to help their children at home, by using commercial materials, were often equally unacceptable to the staff. Teachers argued that providing parents with extra activities might overburden them, or create anxiety, or result in too much pressure on their children.

This was not, however, the parents' view. Despite the intensity of the parent involvement programme, many parents felt that more should have been done to show them how to help their children at home. It was in this sense that they were most interested in being 'involved' in their education. Helping in the class, which the teachers had at the outset of the project seen as a crucial form of involvement, was less popular with the parents. There appeared then, to be not only differences between the values and attitudes of many parents and teachers, but also between their aims for parent involvement.

5

Toy libraries: a case study

Three of the project schools started toy libraries in the course of the programme, only to close them down within a year or two. They had been opened for what seemed very good reasons—the staff believed that some children had very few toys, that most didn't have the kind of toys that would help their development (and which in any case weren't stocked by the local shops), and that the provision of a toy library might encourage the parents to play more with their children. In the event, a large number of toys were broken, or essential parts were lost, while on the other hand many parents were clearly reluctant to use the toy libraries at all.

The school staff naturally felt discouraged, but inquiries in other nursery and infant schools showed that it was common for toy libraries to be under-used. The low income families for whom they were primarily intended seemed particularly disinclined to use them. We suspected that the difficulties arose out of a difference in attitude to toys and play on the part of staff and parents. Teachers usually see play as an important medium for children to learn about the world, develop skills and imagination, and express their feelings. In so far as toys further play, their selection is seen as a serious matter, to be guided by children's developmental needs. This theory assigns to the adult a particular role: he should neither leave the child totally alone nor take over the play, but should join in sufficiently to stimulate play further.

Issues and research findings

People who hold this 'developmental' theory of play prefer toys that encourage creativity. They also tend to see toys as investments, which will give a return over a long time if carefully looked after. Underlying this constellation of attitudes are certain values (planning ahead, investing wisely, valuing creativity, taking responsibility for children's educational needs) historically associated with the middle class.

Not everyone in our society shares these values, or this attitude to play. There are alternative and much older theories, which see play as a way of occupying or amusing children, not of helping them develop. People who hold this view are not likely to consider the choice of toys a very serious matter, and they usually see the adult's role in play as 'all-or-none'. Either the adult works the toys to amuse the child—for example he winds up a clockwork toy—or the child is expected to occupy himself without an adult. Since toys are not bought as long-term investments, they are not expected to last very long, or to need careful attention to ensure their survival.

Of course, many parents buy both 'developmental' and 'occupational' toys—and some toys, such as bicycles, belong to both categories. But toy libraries usually contain only 'developmental' toys. They tend to stock paints, crayons, Lego, bricks, jigsaw puzzles, sorting and threading toys, and games to teach shape and colour (like picture lotto). Most of these toys require an adult's participation, help or supervision. Toy libraries don't contain colouring and 'magic painting' books, clockwork toys, guns, train sets with a fixed lay-out, or Cindy dolls. Nor do they usually contain the big toys which are valued by almost all parents—such as tricycles, and dolls' prams.

One would therefore expect toy libraries to appeal, at the least, to middle class parents, who are likely to share the teachers' values and ideas. But additional complex feelings influence attitudes to toy libraries. Toys are often thought of as *possessions*—a child's first possessions; this stress on ownership is incompatible with the idea of a library. Further, most parents, of whatever social class, think of toys in part as gifts—as extravagant gestures with which to express, sometimes to buy, love. But toys are also bought in response to advertising pressure. Multinational corporations have moved into the toy industry, purveying the message that good parents spend large sums of money on toys. When the child loses interest in his expensive toys, or breaks them, the parent is often left feeling resentful at the waste of money, but aware that he will probably succumb to similar pressures again. Hence toys arouse mixed feelings in many parents, and the notion of a toy library is not always appealing.

To test some of these ideas, we decided to spare our project families another interview and instead to interview mothers in two London nursery schools with toy libraries. In the 'white collar' school half the fathers were white collar workers, the great majority white, and born in the UK. In the 'inner city' school only a fifth of the parents were in white collar jobs, and nearly a half had been born outside the UK, mainly in the West Indies and Spain. Their incomes were often low, and their housing of very poor quality. Most, however, had access to yards where children could play. In each school we interviewed 10 mothers who were regular toy library users, and 10 who were not. There were equal numbers of boys and girls, and three and four year olds, in all groups.

Play with children

Many of the 'white collar' children were clearly getting a lot of attention. 'I pick him up from the nursery at 3.30 each day and devote the next two hours to him, till his father gets back. Not all that time would be spent playing, but he'd be getting all my attention.' An 'inner-city' mother answered rather differently. 'I'm not one of them mothers who run round after their kids all the time. I don't sit down and play with them. They play with each other.' This lack of participation in play did not necessarily mean lack of contact. Another 'inner-city' mother answered

73

'No, I don't play with him much. He plays with the little boy upstairs—they're outside kicking a ball, or making a mess with whatever he's got in that toy box. He likes to help dry the dishes, and carry my shopping. He likes me to read to him.'

When the 'white collar' parents played with their child, it was usually with puzzles, constructional toys, or board and card games, while the 'inner-city' parents most often joined in vigorous play. 'His father pretends to be an elephant and charges at him.' 'He likes us to play hide and seek, and Monsters.' 'We take a bat and ball to the park.' They often commented that the child didn't play much with toys, and preferred to play with other children.

Toys as presents

There were massive differences in the toys given to, and used by the two sexes; these differences were present in both schools, although rather more strongly marked in the inner-city schools. Twice as many boys as girls were said to play with bricks and constructional toys, more than three times as many boys as girls played with transport toys, bicycles, scooters, balls and Action Man; no girls played with guns, shooting ranges, Scalectrix car tracks and electric train sets, and only two boys played with dolls.

In the white collar school the smallest amount spent on Christmas presents for the nursery child was £5, the largest £110 (this was Christmas, 1978). Two thirds of the parents had spent between £5 and £20 on the child, the rest more. In the 'inner-city' school less had been spent. The range was £2.50 to £70; 50 per cent of the parents had spent between £5 and £10 on the child. Only one parent in each school had made a toy, and none had bought second-hand toys.

We asked the mothers how they chose their presents. In both schools just over half the mothers said that they had bought toys that the child had asked for. In the white collar school 65 per cent of mothers said that they had chosen toys that the child 'needed', or would complement his interests or be of value for several years. For example, one mother answered: 'We thought in terms of what he needed, what he was interested in, and what he liked.' Another mother had bought a two-sided easel, so that she and her child could paint together. Few mothers in the inner-city school gave reasons of these kinds. Several had bought on impulse—'I just saw a music-box in the market, and bought it.'

With the exception of one inner-city school child, all the children were given toys as birthday presents. In both schools half the mothers also bought toys or children's books at least once a month.

'Best buys' in toys

We tried to get at the mothers' criteria for judging toys by asking, 'Which is the best toy you have ever bought? Why do you think it was best?' In the white collar school the most frequent choice was construction toys, usually bricks or Lego, but in the inner-city school bikes or tricycles were named most often, followed by dolls and dolls' prams; only three mothers mentioned construction toys. In the white collar school 70 per cent of the mothers gave one or more 'developmental' reason for nominating their best buy. Thus one mother answered: 'Bricks, definitely—they encourage imaginative play, they're versatile, and can be played with at various levels—and you can add to them.' In the inner-city school only 20 per cent of mothers gave reasons of this kind, and the most frequent ground for choice was that a toy kept the child occupied for a long time.

Issues and research findings

Toys for learning

Next we asked 'Have you ever bought toys you think your child will learn from? What were they?' All but one mother in the white collar school answered yes, and several said that they would never buy a toy unless they thought their children could learn from it. The majority added a comment that most play is or can be educational, or that children could learn something from most toys. 'All toys are potentially educational, especially things that help them use their imagination—bricks, for instance; or just finding out what you can do with any toy is educational.'

Seventy-five per cent of the inner-city school mothers said that they had bought educational toys, but they generally used this term to mean instructional toys, mainly jigsaw puzzles and ABC and counting games. 'I suppose what they have at school, puzzles and shapes,' and 'Well, no, he's only three. Next year I might buy him a toy clock or an ABC book.'

The mothers' ambivalence towards toys

When we asked 'How do you feel about toys and games; do you like them?' only half of the mothers in both schools unequivocably answered yes. The remaining 50 per cent of mothers in both schools were evenly divided between those who had mixed feelings and those who positively disliked toys. Typical of the former group was one inner-city mother. 'They need toys—they'd get bored silly otherwise. But sometimes I think they have too many. And lots of toys are rubbish—it's just a racket.' The main objections to toys in both groups were that children had too many and didn't play with them, that they were a nuisance and made the house untidy, and that they were unnecessary, 'He prefers my pots and pans.' 'What they like best is being with people, and chatting.' Some mothers felt that toys were positively harmful because they stopped children using their imaginations, and that the best playthings cost nothing.

We followed this by asking 'Do you think he has enough toys?' All the mothers in the white collar school, and all but three very low income mothers in the inner-city school said yes, and a number added 'far too many'. When we pressed the point further by asking whether there were any toys at all that they would like to buy their children if they could afford to, 90 per cent of mothers in the white collar school said no, but nearly half of the inner-city school mothers *would* have liked to buy other toys—usually expensive ones not stocked by toy libraries— mainly bicycles, pedal cars, and dolls' prams.

Toy library use in the white collar school

It was therefore no surprise that the toy library in the white collar school was not well used. Of the 10 mothers who were said to be regular users, only five had borrowed toys within the past month. We asked the other 15 why they did not make more use of the library, and were most often told that their children had quite enough toys of their own, and that the toy library toys were 'too young'. For example, most puzzles had less than 30 pieces, while at home many of the children tackled much more difficult ones. The games that the parents played with their children at home included draughts, Sorry, Happy Families, Hoopla, and Boules, while most of the toy library games were picture matching games.

Toy library use in the inner-city school

The regular users in this school borrowed toys quite fre- quently—all had used the library within the past month. But half were critical of the selection of toys. 'It's all right, I suppose. They seem to emphasize educational toys, puzzles and that. Jimmy doesn't really want to play with them. The kids go into

Woolworths and see all the attractive toys there, and after that the toy library looks a bit old-fashioned.' 'It's quite all right, but there's not much of a selection. Parents don't want to spend their time helping with blocks and all that.'

We asked the non-users why they did not borrow toys. Seven of the 10 said that they worried about damage and loss. 'I'm afraid he'll spoil them.' 'I don't like lending and borrowing, I'd rather they broke their own toys.' The other three said their children had plenty of toys of their own.

Users and non-users

In the white collar school there was little difference in the social background or in the kind of answers given to our interview questions between users and non-users. But in the inner-city school they formed much more distinct groups. The non-users were more likely to have been born outside the UK; they spent less money on Christmas presents for their children; and their children were less likely to be given toys by friends and relatives. Seven of the 10 mothers said that they would like to give their children more toys, usually bicycles and dolls' prams. These mothers were the ones who did not use the toy library because of anxiety about damage or loss.

The toy library users at the inner-city school tended to make some remark in the course of the interview which showed awareness of the 'development' theory of play. One mother said, 'I'm not one of your middle class mothers, but I watch a lot of TV programmes and read articles. I know that puzzles and paints and Lego help him.' Nine of the ten non-users made no remarks of this kind.

Are toy libraries needed?

In the white collar school in our study, few parents showed much enthusiasm for the library. Three main factors seemed to be responsible—their children were already well supplied with 'developmental' toys, the toys in the library tended to be developmentally too easy for them, and, in addition, many of the mothers had an ambivalent attitude to toys in any case. Although they considered that children needed, and learned from them, they also had an uneasy feeling that their children had too many toys, and didn't play with those they had. In schools like this toy libraries do seem to be unnecessary. It might be useful to arrange toy exhibitions in such schools for first-time parents, but a toy library service can be seen as bringing coals to Newcastle.

The situation is somewhat different in disadvantaged areas. Here, some parents have little money to spend on toys, although others may equip their children with fleets of bicycles and pedal cars. Our interviews in the inner-city school, though, supported our initial expectation that mothers who did not share the teachers' theories about toys would make little use of a toy library, however poor they might be.

Because they expected their children to play on their own or with other children without supervision, their anxiety about possible loss or damage to toys was realistic. They also did not want to harbour toys that required adult help or supervision. Even viewed as a means of occupying children, toys were less important to them than to the white collar mothers; more social activity was usually available to their children, because of larger families and shared yards. Moreover, since their criteria for judging toys were different, the toys supplied by the school looked positively unattractive to them. Jigsaw puzzles and blocks can hardly compete with flashing laser guns and clockwork robots, unless one has a theory about why they are important. Toy library toys are likely to be seen by such parents as in some sense 'educational', assisting in the business of learning shapes, letters, and numbers. But this educational play is seen as a matter for the school; at home a child should be free to amuse himself with his bike, his guns, or with dolls.

It is important not to misinterpret this attitude—it was not generally the case that these parents did not interact with their children, but that they tended to interact with them in the context of housework, social activities and active play. It cannot be assumed that such interactions are less valuable than playing with toys. Teachers who find parents unenthusiastic about their toy library might well consider with the parents alternative ways in which they can help their children's development.

6

One year after intervention

After the two years of intervention we withdrew from the project schools, and had no further contact with them for a year. We were well aware that without the resources of the research team, and the interest of taking part in the project, the teachers' enthusiasm for parent involvement might wane. We planned, therefore, to return to the schools after a year's absence, to discover what activities were still continuing, how parents and staff saw the project in retrospect, and what their present views were about the desirability of parent involvement.

We were able to re-interview six of the seven heads and all seven class teachers. Limited resources prevented us from visiting all the homes again. Instead, we interviewed 42 mothers, six from each unit, of whom three had been amongst the most 'involved' mothers in the class, and three amongst the least involved. By the time of our interviews the children of all these families were in infant school.

In order to allow both mothers and staff to speak their minds more freely than might otherwise have been the case, we arranged for the interviews to be carried out by a community worker who was not part of the project staff.

We started by asking both staff and mothers what, in retrospect, was their opinion of the parent involvement activities which had been organized in their nursery; we also asked the staff whether they were still continuing the activity. Most popular with the mothers were the class book libraries; all the mothers interviewed in the schools which had set them up had used them, and still thought them very worthwhile. The 'open half-hour' was also remembered appreciatively, as were the song and rhyme sheets, especially in one class where the teacher had made attractive folders for the children to keep their weekly sheets in. In fact, only four of the parent involvement activities were commented on critically by any of the mothers—parents' meetings (described by a few as 'a waste of time'); notices to describe and explain the day's activities (one or two mothers said, 'I couldn't understand them,' whilst one or two others said 'nothing new in them'); helping in the class (also thought by some mothers to be 'a waste of time') and toy libraries, which were criticized by the majority of the mothers in the schools which ran them ('he didn't play with them much,' 'it was a headache keeping track of them').

We asked the uninvolved mothers if they had thought the parent involvement activities were uninteresting or not worthwhile. Almost all the mothers rejected these explanations, and said that they hadn't been actively involved in the school because they had had to go to work, or look after a young baby, or hadn't been well.

But the staff had many more reservations than the mothers about the activities. Home visits, song and rhyme sheets and class newsletters were thought worthwhile and had been continued by all the staff who had organized them. The 'open half-hours', which the mothers had liked, were considered an unnecessary disruption of routine and had been stopped, as had the practice of putting up notices to describe and explain the daily nursery activities ('I'm not sure whether anyone read them').

In one or both of the units with the largest proportion of non-indigenous children a number of activities which were continuing elsewhere had been stopped—parents' evenings, helping in the classroom, and book and toy libraries. The staff in these schools felt doubtful whether the activities had achieved their aims, or were worth the time and expense involved.

How much of the programme survived for a year?

Each school had organized between eight and 14 types of activity for parents during the course of the project. One year later, one school had only stopped one of these activities, but on average a third had been stopped. Three of the schools already had an active parent involvement programme before the project began, which had been extended during the project; each of these schools had continued at least one of the new activities. During the year following the end of the project four units started parent involvement activities they had not previously undertaken—for instance an international social evening, a class prospectus.

The activities dropped by the schools seemed to fall under three headings; those requiring resources the schools did not possess, such as video-cameras; those which were expensive to run—like book and toy libraries in the schools where they were lost and damaged; activities primarily aimed at explaining nursery education to parents—for instance the open half-hour, chalked notices explaining the day's activities, evening meetings devoted to explaining the purpose of nursery activities. The teachers had *not* dropped activities simply because they took a lot of effort, or encroached on their free time, provided they were convinced of their value—no one had stopped home-visiting or issuing weekly rhyme and song sheets; the coffee mornings and discussion groups, and the mother and toddler clubs run in the teachers' lunch hours were still flourishing.

When we asked the staff which activity they thought had been the most worthwhile, the majority mentioned occasions which they considered fostered friendly staff-parent relationships: 'home visiting—the relationship you build up is the foundation for everything else that goes on,' 'the mother and toddler club—

the parents learn to trust the teacher before their child starts school,' 'coffee mornings—you get to know the parents better.' Thus, despite the teachers' initial expressed concern to increase parents' understanding of nursery education, it was clear that what they most valued was the development of a feeling of personal trust between teachers and parents.

Did the teachers still want to increase parent involvement?

The fact that in every unit the amount of parent involvement had diminished since the project ended might have been due either to a loss of enthusiasm by the staff or to the loss of the extra resources provided by the project. We therefore asked the staff whether they thought they were now doing about the right amount of work with parents. Two heads thought they were ('We've gone as far as we can') but all the other staff said that they would prefer to do more but found it impossible with their present resources.

What all but one teacher wanted was extra time to talk to parents, either in home visits, or informally in the school. One teacher would have liked to make more films for parents. All the staff felt that the main resource needed for extra work with parents was additional staff. The three units with the most non-indigenous families thought that the best help would be an educational visitor or community liaison teacher who could help them to communicate with minority groups; the others wanted an extra teacher in the school so that they themselves could spend more time with parents: 'I'd like to do 50/50 parent and school work. At present I get an awful guilty feeling when I leave the children.'

Had the parents' enthusiasm continued?

By the time of the interviews the project children were all at infant school. The amount of parent involvement in these schools varied enormously, but in all cases was less than in the project nurseries. We thought it important to establish whether the mothers still wanted to be involved in their children's schooling. It seemed quite possible that they might not see a place for themselves in a 'proper school', or that they might have less time to spare, because they had taken jobs.

One of the most striking features of the project schools had been their openness—any interested parents could watch and have explained to them everything that went on. It was clear that some but not all the mothers felt the lack of this opportunity in the infant schools. Half the mothers said they would like to know more about what went on, and that they didn't know enough about how their children spend their days. Half of the mothers would also have liked to see the nursery involvement programme continued into the infant school, but a fifth definitely didn't want this, usually they said because they were too busy. It was the mothers who had been the most involved in the nursery who wanted the involvement to continue.

The most frequently available forms of involvement open to them in the infant schools were parents' meetings, invitations to help in the classroom, and explanations of how they could help their children at home. It was clear that few of the teachers initiated two-way discussion with the parents—a mother was only asked about her child's out-of-school life if he had been difficult at school. None the less, a third of the mothers said that they would have liked to talk to the teachers about their children's home lives ('She'd know a lot more about him if she did ask') and nearly a half would like the teachers to ask them for suggestions, and for their opinions about school activities ('I don't know if I'd have ideas, but it would be good to be asked').

The proper limits to parent involvement: staff and parent views

The limits of the parent involvement programmes set up in our project were defined not only by what was feasible in the present educational structure, but by what the heads and teachers concerned found acceptable. Modern forms of parent involvement generally involve a departure from the traditional teacher-parent relationships, either in terms of the teacher encroaching on the parent's territory or of allowing the parents to encroach on the teacher's territory.

In our follow-up interviews we tried to discover parents' and teachers' attitudes to these kinds of encroachment. The staff were more enthusiastic than the parents about encroaching on the parent's territory. All but one of the staff thought that teachers should try to influence the way in which parents bring up their children, although a number were anxious to make it clear that they did not want to interfere in the home directly: 'I don't like the word influence—we show by example, or by advice if we're asked,' 'Yes, very subtly, on a one-to-one-basis, and by letting mothers watch us.' Only one teacher dissented: 'Not influence—cooperate. What we do here is not necessarily as good as it could be—parents might have much better ideas.'

Two thirds of the mothers agreed that teachers should try to influence parental child rearing, but a third raised objections: 'That's a difficult one. They're teaching children, but they haven't got any idea of some things—because a lot of them haven't children of their own.' 'No, I think that's wrong. No one knows the children like the parents.'

On the other hand, more mothers than teachers were in favour of parents' encroaching on the teachers' territory. All the mothers were in favour of parents helping in the classroom with non-academic activities (play, and so forth), but two teachers were dubious of the value of this ('Only for my own benefit, when I'm short staffed'). Three quarters of the mothers thought that parents should also help in the classroom with reading and number work, most stressing that they would need supervision: 'If the teacher tells you how to, so that you're not going against her methods,' 'Yes, if it didn't interfere with the teacher's routine it would be great.' Only two of the 13 teachers unequivocally agreed. Four said the questions were not relevant to nursery teachers, three said it depended on the parent: 'Some parents—if there was a regular parent and I knew what their attitudes were,' 'Some of them, parents vary so much,' and four were totally opposed to the idea: 'No—it's difficult to get parents to do things your way,' 'No, they could do more harm than good—they'd have to go to college for three years first.'

Parental assistance in the primary classroom is not uncommon, even though it does arouse controversy. Consulting parents about decisions within the school is very unusual, but we thought it would be worth gauging the reactions of both staff and parents to the idea that parents might be consulted over certain specific issues. The first of these issues was whether parents should be invited to come up with suggestions for schools—for instance, introducing a new activity such as dancing. Nine of the 13 staff thought that they should, although some said that when they asked for suggestions they didn't get any, while others stressed that parents would only make suggestions if they trusted the staff: 'Yes, I aim for my parents to come up with suggestions without feeling they're criticizing me. It can only happen when you've established a good relationship with them.' Four teachers were totally opposed to the notion: 'No, their suggestions are not appropriate. They've got a limited idea of practical difficulties.' Three quarters of the mothers were in favour of the idea: 'Yes, parents can help to vary the routine by suggesting something new.' The rest were doubtful: 'That's a dodgy sort of area—that depends on the teacher.'

Next we asked whether parents should be invited to offer opinions on where to go for school outings. Eight of the 13 staff thought that they should, but the rest demurred: 'No, several of them have weird ideas,' 'They've no idea of the practicalities.' Two thirds of the mothers thought parents should be asked for their opinions: 'Parents would have ideas, because they take their own children out.'

Fewer staff (five out of 13) thought that parents should be consulted about a third issue, school hours and holiday dates. The majority argued that it would be pointless, since they would all have different ideas. Half of the mothers thought that parents should be consulted on this issue—most of them wanted to put forward their opinion that the summer holidays are too long. The same proportion of staff, five out of 15, were prepared to listen to parents' opinion on the curriculum, for instance whether 'new maths' should be taught, or whether nursery children should be taught to write their names: 'I'd be prepared to discuss with the mothers. I'd tell them my reasons, and justify them, but in the end I'd decide.' The majority again thought these matters were the preserve of teachers. 'No, you'd get on terribly sticky ground. That's what the teacher is being paid for.' Just under half the parents would like to be asked for opinions on the curriculum: 'Yes, for instance I think they should start reading earlier,' but the majority parent opinion, was summed up by one mother—'No, teachers are trained to know these things.'

Five of the 13 staff also thought that parents' opinions should be sought on school rules—for instance whether sweets should be allowed in school. 'If you have a good core of parents you can discuss these questions with them,' 'I'd invite opinions, and if someone came up with a better solution I'd consider it.' The majority staff opinion, however, was: 'No, parents views are too diverse. The running of the school should be left to the staff.' Just under half the mothers thought parents should be consulted about school rules: 'Yes, because the school ought to reflect what we're doing and not go against us at home,' but again, the majority argued 'No, that would undermine the teacher's authority.'

Finally, we asked whether parents' views should be sought on the selection of teaching staff. Two of the 13 staff thought this would be acceptable *via* parent governors, but for the rest: 'That's going too far, parents aren't here long enough to make that sort of decision,' 'No, that's a professional matter.' Only four of the 42 mothers thought that parents should be consulted on this issue—one Asian mother thought that it might lead to the appointment of more Asian teachers, and the other three thought that parent representatives should sit on selection committees. The rest answered 'No, parents don't know what qualifications are required,' 'Definitely not, I'm quite happy to trust their judgement.'

In each case we also asked both parents and staff whether they thought parents should be involved in decision-making, as well as discussion. Two of the staff thought that parents could take part in making all these decisions, via parent governors. A fifth of the mothers thought that parents should take part in every decision except the selection of staff, which only 10 per cent thought should be a matter for parents.

While we found little evidence then, that parents want to 'take over' schools, we did find that about half the parents would like to be asked for their opinions and suggestions about school matters. The other half of the parents interviewed argued that what went on inside the school was the teachers' business, and should be left to trained professionals. The proportion of mothers who wanted to be consulted was about the same in middle class and working class areas, and mothers who had not been involved in the nursery programmes were just as likely to consider they should be consulted as the highly involved mothers. The evidence suggested, in fact, that there were two distinct but overlapping groups of parents; those who wanted to be involved in activities organized by the school, and those who would like the teachers to listen to their opinions on school matters.

About the same proportion of teachers as parents agreed, at least in principle, that parents should be asked for their opinions. There was, in fact, a surprising match in this respect on each question asked. How far these attitudes are representative of teacher and parent opinion generally it is impossible to say. Since the teachers had volunteered to take part in the project, and both teachers and parents had taken part in the parent involvement programme, it seems unlikely that their views are entirely typical.

Do staff and parents want to be on closer terms?

One of the hallmarks of the professional is that he prefers to keep a certain social distance between himself and his client. There are complex advantages in this tradition; it may enhance his status, enable him to make more objective professional judgements, and allow him to protect himself emotionally from too many demands from his clients.

At the same time, this very distance precludes the intimate knowledge of his clients and uninhibited social exchange with them which some professionals feel to be important. Teachers, for example, often say that their relationships with their pupils greatly improve when they get to know them in an out-of-school setting such as a school camp. The playgroup movement sees as one of its strengths the friendly equal relations between leader and parents. Personal friendship between staff and parents is unusual in urban schools: indeed, Eric Midwinter has described the journey of teachers to school as a process of 'riding through enemy-occupied territory at 9 a.m. to man foreign legion type fortresses'.

In our follow-up interview we thought it worth asking both staff and parents about the degree of intimacy they considered desirable between teachers and parents. One traditional preserve of the teacher is the staffroom, from which both parents and children are usually excluded. We had found in our project that parents helping in the school usually resented being excluded from the staffroom at coffee-time, so we asked both parents and staff whether they thought this practice was correct. Two of the heads thought it was necessary to protect the staff's privacy, but all the other teachers and all but four parents thought it was impolite. Some parents also saw visiting the staffroom as a chance to get to know the staff better.

There was, indeed, evidence of a widespread desire amongst the parents to get to know the staff. All but five of the mothers said that they would like to invite the teachers to their homes for a social visit, but in only three instances had this happened. The same 37 mothers said that they would like to visit the teachers' homes if they were invited, some adding, 'I'd love to, but I've never been asked,' 'It would be a privilege.' Only two mothers had in fact visited a teacher at home. Those who demurred generally argued 'That's going a bit too far. They would be overloaded with mothers.'

This tended also to be the point of view of the teachers. Only five said that they would like to invite the parents to their homes, and had done so on occasion, six said that they had thought about it, but had not done so: 'You'd have to be careful of favouritism,' 'If you did it for one, you'd have to do it for all,' and two heads answered: 'No, parents would feel alien in my home,' 'No, I'm too busy.'

As for visiting the homes of the parents, seven staff said that they had occasionally done so, or said that they would in principle accept an invitation, but they had never been asked; one said that she would refuse, in order to avoid favouritism; the rest were doubtful. 'I suppose if I were asked I'd accept. But I wouldn't really want to be asked. If you started with one you'd have to go on to all. Friends are separate from school—we have our own lives to lead.'

Finally, we asked both staff and parents if they would like to be on first name terms. Only six of the 42 parents were in favour of this; the main objections were that their children would not respect the teacher if they heard their parents use her first name, or that it would diminish the teacher's status: 'No, I wouldn't like that, it's a good idea to hold teachers a little in respect,' 'No, not in front of the children. They might treat teachers like ordinary friends.' Two mothers commented that it was all right to call nursery teachers by their first names, but that in the primary school discipline had to be maintained.

Three of the teachers liked the idea of being on first name terms with the parents, but the views of the others were expressed by one teacher: 'No, I've always wanted to keep the idea that I'm a "teacher", not a pal. I like to keep work and private life separate. In front of the children, I prefer the authority of a surname.'

The majority of the mothers then, would have liked to get to know the teachers better than is generally the case at present, but did not want to be on too familiar terms with them, for fear of diminishing the teacher's authority. There were no differences in the proportion of involved and uninvolved mothers, or mothers from middle class and working class schools, who held these views: not so many staff wanted to get to know the parents better; they were inclined to think that greater intimacy might lead to jealousy between parents, as well as to an infringement of their own privacy.

The staff's view of the research project

We were well aware that the research project made considerable demands on the teaching staff. In the schools on which we concentrated, the research officers spent two days a week in the school, took up the teacher's lunch hour once a week for discussion, and exerted a steady pressure on the staff to set up and monitor activities. We took up much less of the headteachers' time, but they had to tolerate outsiders visiting their schools and suggesting changes in school practice.

We ended, then, by asking the staff how they felt about their participation in the project. The response of all the staff was mixed; seven stressed gains, while six were more eloquent about the difficulties. The class teachers were more positive than the heads. They had all found the project stimulating: 'It made me think a lot more. I was under pressure to get on and achieve what I was trying to do, because the research officer was visiting to see the results,' 'It was extremely interesting to have what we were doing monitored and discussed,' 'We all learnt a great deal.' Those teachers who were inclined to minimize the difficulties described the main snags as the extra paper-work, or the disruption of nursery routine involved in introducing the research officer's suggestions. The teachers who stressed problems came either from units where the project had led to friction within the school (with the head, nursery assistant or other staff) or where the research staff had greatly reduced their contacts with them in the second year.

Despite our initial anxiety that the teachers might find it irksome to have research officers in their classrooms for two days a week, in two units the staff said that they would have liked the research officer to spend *more* time in the school, and in another two they thought that two days a week was about right. The staff in the three units where, after the first year, we made only occasional visits had felt the loss of contact strongly: 'We needed someone all the time, or nothing.' One teacher understandably resented the ending of the project. She felt that the research staff, by providing extra resources for two years and then withdrawing them, had used her for their own purposes. Nevertheless, she felt she had gained something from the experience.

Twice-termly discussion meetings were held throughout the project for all research and teaching staff. About 20 people were usually present; some made a long journey to London at the end of the school day. Seven staff were enthusiastic about the meetings, without any reservations: 'I did enjoy them, especially meeting people from other areas.' Five staff had some reservations—that the group was too large, with the result that staff felt anxious, and could not talk freely, or that there was 'a lot of waffle', and not enough discussion of practicalities. One teacher thought that her efforts were not appreciated, because the special problems of her school were not well enough understood. Everyone thought the meetings occurred with about the right frequency.

Conclusion

It was certainly not the case that the research project had exhausted the interest of staff and parents in parent involvement. A year after the end of our intervention most of the parents remembered the activities with enthusiasm, about half would have liked them to continue into the infant school, and about half would have liked the infant teachers to seek their opinions on school activities. As to the staff, while the number of parent involvement activities they organized had decreased, it was still larger than before the project started. Further, all the teachers would have liked to increase the amount of work they did with parents.

The extent to which the research staff had altered the teachers' attitudes was less clear. Throughout the project we had argued that parent involvement could be a two-way process, with the staff seeking ideas, opinions, and information from the parents. Initially, most of the staff had received this argument with scepticism; their view of parent involvement was essentially of a one-way process, with the teacher informing and attempting to influence the parents.

During the course of the project several teachers did begin to listen to parents and to encourage their initiative in their schools, and one year later half of the staff said that they thought parents should be consulted on a variety of school issues. But at this stage only one teacher was putting these views into practice. Others may have been constrained by opposition from heads and colleagues, but there was some evidence that the main shift in their attitude was from an initial desire for parents to *understand* what went on in school to a greater emphasis on the need to develop friendly staff-parent relationships.

It had become clear during the project that increasing parental understanding was not always easy. It seemed that the staff now hoped to circumvent this step, by developing personal trust in themselves and by this means influencing parents and gaining support for their work. (See Chapter 7, pages 110–11 for further discussion of this point.) In at least one of the schools with a large proportion of non-indigenous parents, it was also true that the staff became more aware during the project of their need for help in contacting and understanding the local community.

7

Some underlying difficulties

The aim we set ourselves in this project was to analyse the attitudes of teachers and parents to parent involvement in nursery education, and to throw light on the problem of why such programmes are more successful in some areas than others. In the preceding chapters we have described the impact of the programmes we helped to set up in seven nursery units. We assessed this impact in terms of the proportion of parents involved, the extent to which the teachers' aims in organizing the activities were achieved, and the teachers' and parents' view of the programme. In this chapter we will draw together the threads of our discussion, and attempt to analyse the reasons for the successes and failures we encountered.

The distinction between cooperation and involvement

The point has already been made that any discussion of parent involvement is deeply confused by the variety of meanings given to the term. It is not simply that it is an imprecise term, but that it is used in totally different ways. A school which is said to have 'a lot of parent involvement' may be one with an active parent-teacher association, one which organizes successful fund-raising activities, or one in which every classroom has parents

helping children with academic work. Further, parent involvement is advocated for many different reasons, ranging from a
wish to mobilize extra resources for the school to a belief that
parents have a right to be involved in decision taking. Part of the
uneasiness which many teachers undoubtedly feel about parent
involvement stems from their awareness that the term *does* carry
this wide range of meanings, not all of which they find acceptable.

The discussion may be clarified by considering the distinc-
tion between cooperation and involvement. Traditional home-
school cooperation, as we pointed out at the beginning of this
book, involves the parents' showing active, informed support
for the school by providing the kind of back-up teachers want—
raising funds, attending open days, seeing that homework is
done, helping children with the kind of reading and leisure
interests that will further their education. For their part, the
teachers' decisions tend to be influenced by an awareness of the
parents' wishes—whether these relate to the desirability of
school uniform or the need for rapid progress with academic
work.

This model of parent cooperation is characterized by a strict
demarcation of roles—parents do not expect to help in the class,
or be consulted in decision-making, and equally staff do not
expect to visit parents at home or offer them advice on child
rearing. It is also characterized by the implicit quality of the
staff-parent understanding—the staff do not formally consult
parents about their wishes, the parents do not need to be told
which kinds of reading material and out-of-school experiences
they should provide for their children.

There is no doubt that many teachers would prefer traditional parent cooperation to modern forms of parent involvement. Yet what they tend to overlook is that traditional cooperation depends on staff and parents having shared values and
shared experiences; it is for this reason that explicit communication about what each is expected to contribute is unnecessary.
Further, it depends on the parents' trust in the school as an

institution—their belief that the school will do everything possible to equip their children for the kind of future they want for them.

Cooperation of this kind is therefore unrealizable in any setting where teachers and parents do not have shared values and similar cultural and educational backgrounds, and where parents do not have trust in the school as an institution which will do the best for their child. Thus, it is unlikely to occur in most working class areas, or in areas where staff and parents come from very different cultures. In these areas, teachers must either decide to manage without the kind of parental support they would like, or as our project teachers did, evolve methods of explicitly involving parents in the school. But these methods can never achieve the traditional state of parent cooperation; instead, they inevitably raise the problems associated with parent involvement.

Other teachers and parents may reject the traditional model of parent cooperation as inadequate, precisely because it *does* depend on implicit communication and a clear demarcation of roles. They may see parent involvement as a way of enriching the school by enlisting the skills and knowledge of the parents, benefiting children by improved school-home liaison, and satisfying the desire of many parents to assist in their children's education. They may also consider that parents should have some influence on decisions made within the school.

But for whatever reasons parent involvement is sought, there are certain underlying difficulties likely to arise, which occurred in our project, and are discussed further in this chapter.

Problems arising from a lack of resources

1 Lack of appropriate training in working with parents

Teachers are usually not taught how to explain their work to parents, how to organize untrained volunteers in their classroom, run workshops and discussion groups for parents, or suggest ways in which parents can help their children at home. These activities call for different skills from managing a classroom, or working with an individual child; the teacher must also become something of a community worker and an adult education tutor. Not surprisingly, many teachers are daunted by this prospect. In the course of our project we produced materials designed to help them, some of which are included in the second part of this book.

2 Lack of appropriate training in evaluation

Few teachers have been trained to assess the effectiveness of the practices they introduce. Of course, they usually know how many parents take part in any particular parent activity ('it's always the same ones'), but they are much less likely to know why the other parents didn't take part, whether the activity fulfilled the aim for which it was intended, and what proportion of parents haven't taken part in any parent activity. Yet without this information their efforts may be misdirected. For example, one teacher thought that her toy library was not much used because the parents now bought similar toys for their children; when interviewed, the parents said that they didn't use the library because they thought the toys were too babyish for their children. Teachers may believe that parents don't attend meetings because they are lacking in confidence or uninterested in education, when the reason the parents give is that the meetings are uninteresting.

Admittedly, teachers don't have time to interview parents at home or issue questionnaires, but there are a variety of simple ways of getting some feedback, ranging from informal discussions with small groups of parents, to asking for written opinions on a particular questions to be put in a suggestion box.

3 Lack of resources

Nursery and infant schools usually lack even the most primitive means of mass producing attractive written or visual materials for parents; most teachers lack access to interpreters and translators to help them communicate with non-English-speaking parents. Most important of all, teachers lack time to work with parents, especially at an individual level. Time spent in organizing parent help, preparing for, and carrying out individual consultations, paying home visits, or holding discussion groups, must be taken from time that would otherwise be devoted to the children, or from the teacher's free time.

Nursery school teachers are expected not only to work with children but also to organize the work of nursery assistants, and to train students in the classroom. If in addition they are expected to give time to parents, conscientious teachers will inevitably feel torn between these various claims.

It is true that in principle the presence of parent volunteers in the classroom should enable teachers to devote more time to children. But briefing and deploying volunteers, and keeping them happy and feeling useful, requires managerial skills which don't come easily to all teachers.

4 Lack of appropriate role definition

A related problem is that of how the teacher and the education authorities define the teaching role. Generally, the teacher's role is seen as working with children. Work with parents, although paid lip service by authorities, is rarely given priority either in teacher training or in any subsequent assessment of the teacher's work. In fact, college tutors, heads, and advisors, are likely to give more weight to the quality of the young teacher's wall displays than to her attempts to foster relationships with parents. Hence she is likely to feel not only role conflict, but guilt, if she devotes much of her time to parents.

5 Lack of adequate time, knowledge and resources to make activities for parents appealing

Turning out at night to attend meetings at school is often not an attractive proposition to parents, and this may also be true of spending time in the classroom. We found that parents often felt ill-at-ease in the classroom setting, uncertain of their role in relation to both staff and children. A mother who can confidently help her children to make jam tarts at home will not necessarily feel this confidence when given the same task inside the classroom. For example, at home she may insist that the children complete the task, and produce tarts of an acceptable quality, but she may notice that at school the teacher does not insist on children completing a task. Similarly, the teachers' disciplinary methods may be very different from her own. We found that many middle class mothers, the majority of whom were sufficiently convinced of the importance of nursery activities to want to help in the class, shared these reservations. Parents' meetings are often about very general topics, such as 'the development of play', which are likely to be treated much more vividly and successfully in television programmes. Discussions about individual children may be couched in such vague or discouraging terms ('she's doing very well', 'he's rather lazy', 'she doesn't seem to mix well') that parents may not find them rewarding, or the effort of turning out to hear them may not seem worthwhile.

6 Lack of adequate knowledge about how to influence parents

Almost all the project teachers wanted to influence aspects of parents' behaviour, and believed that this could be most effectively done by inviting them into the school, to watch the staff and see the play activities provided. About half of the parents in the indigenous schools said that they *had* been influenced in this way—mainly in the direction of allowing the child more 'messy' play activities at home. This was certainly a change favoured by the teachers, but there was apparently no other change in home activities that they wished to encourage—such as joint imaginative and constructional play, or child-centred 'educational' outings.

This failure is hardly surprising, since if parents are to learn by watching teachers the first requirement is that the teacher should 'model' the behaviour the parent is to copy. But nursery teachers don't in fact offer such a model. They tend, from the nature of their job, to spend their time organizing and initiating activities, moving from one child to another, and working with groups of children. If the parents *were* to be influenced by watching school activities, what they would usually see is children playing with each other, and with 'messy activities', not staff playing with children, taking them on outings, or, with some exceptions, reading to them individually. To offer parents a model of what they want them to do at home, the staff would have to change what *they* do at school, and devote more time to playing and reading with individual children.

The feasibility of this approach was shown in the 'book campaigns' in two indigenous schools. In these schools a modelling situation was set up—the class was entirely given over to books for an hour, and both staff and parents read individually to children. This did seem to lead to an increase in the frequency of parents reading through books to children at home. A similar method could be used to encourage parents to play with their children, if this was considered important. For example, the teacher could organize a 'games' hour when games such as picture dominoes were set out and staff and parents sat down and played with the children, or a 'construction' hour, when staff and parents helped children to build with materials such as Lego.

However, even if the teacher does offer a model to parents, they will only change their behaviour if motivated to do so. The teachers implicitly assumed that parents would like what they saw, and wish to copy it. But not all parents enjoy playing with children, other than physical play, or consider it a valuable way to spend their time. This is particularly likely to be the case with parents from very different cultures, for instance Asian and Caribbean families. The majority of non-indigenous parents in our project said they had *not* been influenced by watching in the nursery; either they did not like what they saw, or they considered it too remote from their lives at home to be relevant. These mothers may involve young children in work more often than play. Helping an adult with housework can present young children with very valuable learning experiences; learning to wind up a flex on a vacuum cleaner or to chop vegetables is more demanding than many nursery activities. We found that most parents would welcome guidance about how to help their children, but it seems likely that to be acceptable this help should involve parents in activities which they enjoy and consider important.

Problems arising from communication difficulties

1 With parents from a different culture

The problem we have just discussed is an example of the difficulties which may arise in communication between staff and parents of different cultures, especially when they are unfamiliar with each other's culture. This is because not only some of their values, but also their conceptions of childhood, parenthood, play, toys, and schooling are likely to differ.

Cultural differences of this kind are not always obvious. Teachers may assume that parents don't read to their children or play with them because they can't afford books and toys. But the parents may see their role in bringing up children quite differently, and expect their children to amuse themselves. Hence, even if they are lent books and toys by the school, they may leave their children to look at and play with them on their own. Or teachers may assume that if only the parents will come and watch what is going on in the nursery, they will appreciate the value of nursery education. But parents who put a high value on hard work, obedience and cleanliness are not likely to respond favourably to the sight of children playing at the sand-tray. The children's art work which delights the teachers may be seen as daubs of paint by parents with a different taste in art. These problems are, of course, intensified if teacher and parents don't have a common language. It is not surprising that the teachers in our project from schools with a large proportion of non-indigenous parents became discouraged by failures of com-munication, and generally abandoned attempts to run evening meetings, toy libraries, and even book libraries.

Cultural differences are also present, although less pro-nounced, between teachers and staff in schools in indigenous working class areas. We found that parents in these schools tended to prefer factual books to the story books favoured by the staff, and to show less appreciation of imaginative play and creative art work than did the staff. They were more interested than the staff in their children acquiring specific skills, like swimming, and were concerned that they should learn to settle down to work. They tended to see their own role primarily in terms of fostering their children's moral and social develop-ment, while both the teachers and the middle class parents stressed the parents' role in furthering intellectual develop-ment.

2 With parents from a different educational background

A less serious, but none-the-less real barrier to communication can be the difference in the educational background of staff and parents. Successful communication between any two persons depends on a substratum of shared ideas and experiences. The success of our project teachers' attempts to explain their aims, and the purposes of nursery activities, related directly to the educational level of the parents they were dealing with. In the most middle class school the parents were already familiar with such terms as 'language development', 'imagination' and 'mathematical concepts'. They also shared some very general theories about development and knowledge with the staff. Thus, even though they may initially not have known that for instance the teachers considered that water and sand play developed an understanding of the properties of matter, they quickly grasped these explanations once they were made. Parents with less previous exposure to these concepts, and unfamiliar with modern theories of development and learning, were at best likely to gather that the teacher believed that children in some way learned through playing with sand. They were also likely to continue to see nursery education in terms of a series of specific activities—learning to paint, to sing rhymes, and so forth—whilst the teachers saw these activities as means of developing language or creativity.

A communication gap between laymen and professionals is unavoidable, and not easily overcome by a brief verbal explanation. For example, the extent to which the patient grasps the doctor's explanation of his illness is determined by his prior knowledge of anatomy, physiology, the germ theory of disease, and so on. The extensive adult education material which is nowadays presented in the mass media (for instance in programmes for parents) is tending to close the gap. Nevertheless the process of giving information to parents in a form which they can assimilate is not as straightforward as it seems. This is not to say that it is impossible, but only that it is likely to take considerable time and thought.

Problems arising from teachers' and parents' beliefs in professionalism

A central tenet of 'professionalism' is the belief that, because of the professional's specialist knowledge, critical comments on his work cannot be made by laymen. Only other professionals are considered competent to evaluate and judge his work. Further, since each profession tries to prevent laymen from encroaching on its territory, it is considered unacceptable for a professional to share or teach his professional skills to laymen, or to allow laymen to carry out his tasks. In order to maintain professional status, it is also considered unacceptable for the professional to admit ignorance to the layman, or to ask him for opinions or advice. For the same reason it is often believed advisable to maintain an element of social distance in professional-lay relationships—for instance separate dining rooms, even separate lavatories, may be provided for professionals and laymen.

Professionalism is perhaps found at its least challenged in medicine. Admission to the profession is difficult, public disagreements are rare, self diagnosis and medication is frowned on, medical work may only be evaluated by other doctors, and a decision which a doctor labels a 'clinical judgement' is difficult even for other doctors to challenge. The professional status of the teacher is less secure: this may be because entry to the profession is easier, its social standing is lower, and its claim to esoteric knowledge weaker. Despite, or perhaps because, of this, the teachers' professionalism is in some ways more extreme than that of other professions. For example, the architect's client is expected to describe in considerable detail the kind of building he wants; the architect's skill resides in knowing how to carry through these ideas, given the resources available. Many doctors see it as part of their role to advise the patient on the rival merits of alternative treatments for a particular condition, and then to help the patient to receive the treatment of her choice.

Teachers, on the other hand, do not expect to be guided by their clients (their pupils, parents, or even the school governors), about their aims for the school, or their aims for a particular child. There are, of course, constraints on them from the structure of the examination system, and the visits of inspectors and advisors, but there are no expectations within the educational system that the client should be involved in these decisions.

This situation creates no fundamental difficulties for traditional parent-staff cooperation, where there is implicit agreement between staff and parent on aims and methods, and parents do not encroach on the teacher's role. But it inevitably raises problems for teachers considering parent involvement. None of the staff in our project exhibited an extreme degree of professionalism, or they would not have volunteered to take part in the research. However, professionalism was to a varying extent an important influence on them all. This was evidenced both by their selection of parent involvement activities, and by their answers to our follow-up questions about what limits of parent involvement are desirable. These questions were often met by a blanket answer: 'That's a professional matter', or by reference to the parent's lack of knowledge—'They'd need three years at college first.'

A belief that parents are not entitled to discuss the curriculum was probably responsible for the reluctance of the parents to put forward their view that the children were 'playing around' in the nursery, and the reluctance of the staff to encourage such discussions. Even consulting parents about minor educational decisions, such as the selection of books, or choice of outings, was often considered unprofessional. The refusal of the infant school heads who were approached in our project to allow groups of parents to visit their schools, and discuss what they had seen, in part reflected the professional attitude that their work should not be discussed and evaluated by laymen. The feeling that skill-sharing is unprofessional was one reason why staff did not like the idea of writing or reading workshops, to show parents how to help their children at home. For the same reason, while all of our staff encouraged parents to help in the classroom, most of them thought that this help should not extend to 'early reading' and 'early mathematics' activities.

An underlying belief that as professionals they were adequately equipped to teach their class probably contributed to the reluctance of most of the teachers to recognize that parents had anything special to offer the school.

Consequently, parents were usually asked to help with routine nursery activities, rather than contribute their own skills and knowledge. Much nursery and infant education is centred round themes, such as 'people's jobs', 'pets'. The material for these is usually culled from books, yet, as the Newsons (1977) have pointed out, 'It seems strange that teachers do not attempt to tap the real-life experience of the coalface workers, lathe operators, lorry drivers and bricklayers who are their children's own fathers, many of whom work shifts which would allow them to bring their knowledge into school.'

The same inability to acknowledge the parents' expertise about their own children seemed to underlie the lack of enthusiasm of most of the teachers for organizing individual two-way exchanges of opinion and information with parents. The need to uphold professional status by creating social distance between themselves and the parents prevented some of them from asking parents into the staffroom, and most of them from developing out-of-school relationships with them. The advantages of this social distance for the teachers are obvious, but a serious disadvantage is that it tends to prevent them from knowing much about the children's families, their lives out-of-school, and the local community. Hence they are likely to be unaware of what parents are doing for and with their children, and what they could contribute to the school.

It is also the case that a belief in professionalism prevents many parents from supporting parent involvement. These parents argue that what goes on in school is the business of the teachers, and should be left to them, and that they themselves lack the training to assist in the school or offer suggestions or opinions. They may equally object to other parents taking these roles.

Some parents whose children attend playgroups transfer them to a nursery class if a place becomes available, because of the value that they attach to professional care. Parent-run community nurseries may find that some parents would prefer trained nurses to run the nursery. This point of view is very acceptable to many teachers. Yet when held by parents who know little about the educational system, and understand neither the teachers' aims and methods, nor how to give the children the educational back-up expected by teachers, it cannot lead to the implicit support they would wish. The price that the teacher pays for the parents' belief in professionalism may therefore be an apathetic, even hostile, parent body. We found that non-indigenous parents often combined a critical attitude to the school with a belief in professionalism. They did not much like what the teacher did, but considered that schooling was a matter for trained teachers, and not their concern. Many of them would have liked to resolve this dilemma by sending their child to a fee paying school more to their liking.

Other problems from the parents' point of view

1 Lack of time and energy

Any form of parent involvement that requires the parent to visit the school, either during the day or the evening, is taxing for working mothers, or women with babies or large families. This was a major problem in the project schools with a large proportion of non-indigenous parents. Quite apart from problems of cultural differences or lack of a common language, the parents in these schools had very little time to spare.

2 Lack of power within the school setting

If a teacher's aim for parent involvement is to encourage parents to play an active role within the school, and especially to put forward ideas and suggestions, she may well be frustrated. Not all parents accept that it is best to 'leave it to the teacher', but they may still be reluctant to offer opinions.

A parent's relationship to a teacher is very different from her relationship to a playgroup leader. The leader has been appointed by a parent committee, which is responsible for all the major decisions in the group. Margaret McMillan may have urged teachers to regard parents as 'sovereigns, if not rulers' of the nursery school (page 28) but her successors have not been disposed to see parents in this light. In most schools there are no structures through which parents as a group can be consulted, and parents can only raise issues with teachers on an individual basis. (Parent governors are rarely briefed by, or report back to, the parent body.)

They may well be reluctant to take this step. Little is gained by putting forward opinions and suggestions if they are not likely to be acted on; moreover, much may be lost, if the teacher is antagonized. But putting forward opinions and suggestions in such a way that they are not received as hostile criticisms is a difficult social skill. As one of our project teachers pointed out, parents are not likely to attempt this exercise unless they have a good personal relationship with the teacher, and are confident that she will not take offence. Parents cannot afford to offend teachers—they have surrendered a hostage in the shape of their child. Hence the parents' apparent passivity may simply reflect a realistic appreciation of their role in the school.

The success of parent involvement in different areas

Like others, we found that parent involvement programmes were most successful in our most middle class school. If the analysis we have presented is accepted, the reasons are clear. Teachers and parents to a large degree shared similar values and a common cultural background, very few mothers worked full-time, most had labour saving devices or domestic help which gave them some leisure, and because they themselves had been successful in the educational system most felt reasonably self confident in their relations with the teacher. In the 'Asian' and multi-racial units these conditions tended not to be present, and the teachers often felt discouraged by the failure of their attempts to involve parents.

It was, of course, possible that the success of the parent involvement programme in the most middle class school depended on the success of the staff in maintaining the limits they wished to set to the programme. The head was anxious to see that parents 'did not go too far'. Any contribution they made to the school was closely directed if not actually initiated by the staff. Equally there was little indication that the parents wished to exceed these limits; they were impressed by the expertise of the teacher, and noted that she did in fact tend to respond to their wishes (for instance to start to teach the children to read) without any open discussion of the matter.

An alternative to structured parent involvement: personal trust

On our return visit to the schools a year after the completion of the intervention a particular pattern of 'dropped' activities was discernable. The teachers tended to have abandoned formal efforts to explain nursery activities to parents, (*via* posters, meetings, 'open sessions') and to be making much less effort to persuade parents to help in the class or to use the toy and book libraries. On the other hand they tended to have retained, and hoped to increase, opportunities for social contacts with parents—coffee mornings, home visits, mother and toddler clubs, social evenings.

Behind this pattern seemed to be an awareness of the problems inherent in attempting to explain nursery activities and influence parent-child interactions when the parents came from a very different background from their own. Instead, they hoped to develop personal trust between staff and parents. Good staff-parent relationships were naturally very rewarding to the teachers. They saw them as the most valuable aspect of the intervention. In effect, what they hoped for the future was to achieve the mutual trust and support which characterizes the traditional model of parent cooperation while shedding most of the trappings of modern parent involvement.

Whether this decision was a sensible compromise or an impossible aspiration would require a further exercise in evaluation to determine. Our own belief was that the trust which developed during the project was a by-product of the intensiveness of the parent involvement programme. The parents were impressed by the teacher's efforts on their behalf, and by the fact that everything in the school was open, and explained to them. We felt uncertain whether the trust would have developed solely on the basis of informal conversations.

Nevertheless, the teachers were certainly right in stressing the importance of good personal relationships with parents. They were also right in their belief that these were likely to be fostered by meeting them in informal settings, in the parents' homes for instance, on outings, or at social evenings. But although friendly relationships may make it easier to work with parents, they won't in themselves achieve the aims of parent involvement programmes. For the teacher who wants parents to understand what she is trying to achieve, to provide her with the kind of back-up she wants and to exchange views and information with her, informal contacts are not enough.

Possible solutions to the problems of parent involvement

The first set of problems which we outlined above are relatively simple to solve in *principle*, by affecting changes in teacher training, and by the allocation of extra resources. At Belfield School, in Lancashire, the nursery class has two teachers, each of whom devotes half her time to the class, the other half to work with parents (Garvey, 1975). This arrangement provides extra resources and an unambiguous role definition, and enables contacts to be made with parents who can't manage to visit the school. Doubling the staff ratio is clearly an unrealistic aim at the present time. But freeing class teachers to work with parents for half a day a week would open more possibilities to them. Parent involvement activities *can* be appealing; we discuss ways of making them attractive and interesting in the second part of this book.

The problems which arise from a lack of shared education and culture between staff and parents, and from professionalism, are much more difficult to tackle. Our attempts to help the teachers to explain the principles and practice of nursery education only succeeded with those parents who were already familiar with the underlying concepts. It seemed to us that intensive work with individual parents, focused on a discussion of the present functioning of their own children and the developments that could be expected during the next year, would be the best way to familiarize parents with developmental concepts. Such an undertaking would, again, require extra teacher time, as well as changes in teacher training.

Differences in educational level may hinder parents from giving informed support to the staff, but cultural differences can lead to a more profound distrust. Schools with a large proportion of parents from a very different culture tend either to ignore the differences altogether, or to incorporate acceptable aspects of the parents' culture into the school—for instance Asian food, West Indian steel bands—while ignoring aspects which the staff find 'unacceptable'. But it is the 'unacceptable' aspects that parents often regard as much the most important. For example, Asian parents may be more concerned that their children are taught to sit still, work hard and be respectful to their elders than that Asian food should be provided at the school parties.

Rather than ignore value differences between staff and parents it would be possible for the staff to confront them openly in discussion, and hope to persuade parents either to alter their point of view, or to arrive at an acceptable compromise. At the present time however, there is no mechanism in most schools by which parents *can* put forward their point of view, and discuss it with the staff, except on an individual basis. Parent-teacher associations rarely fulfil this role, and the appointment of one or two parent governors does not in itself promote discussion between staff and parents.

It might be argued that a marked disparity between the values of parents and staff should lead not only to discussion between them, but to a greater degree of influence by parents over the decisions made within the school. This would imply either that parents should play a major role within the management of the school, or that there should be a more pluralistic educational system, which would allow parents to patronize or set up the kind of school they wanted. This could be organized either through an educational voucher scheme, or by providing funds for community or religious groups to run their own schools.

Within the framework of our present system, teachers have the alternative of ignoring value differences, or attempting, to increase communication between staff and parents, in the hope that agreement or compromise will follow greater mutual understanding. The difficulty of such communication has already been discussed; our experience suggests that it is more likely to take place outside the school setting. Teachers often complain that parents rarely come to school, yet they themselves don't visit the families at home, and are often unfamiliar with the shops, cafes, and meeting places of the local community. School meetings held in the nearby temple might not only attract many parents, but also indicate that the school was prepared to go to unusual lengths to contact parents. The appointment of minority group members to senior positions in the schools would also facilitate discussion between staff and parents.

Another approach might be to appoint a neutral person, less strongly associated with school than a teacher, to visit parents and mediate between home and school. A number of authorities have, in fact, appointed educational visitors, or home liaison teachers. But their function is usually seen as explaining the school's educational programme to the parents and trying to persuade them to provide what the staff consider appropriate support—reading to children, buying them educational toys, and so on.

This job description makes sense if the aim of the educational authority is to influence and help parents. If, however, their aim is to improve home-school relationships by bringing the views and the resources of the parents to the school, as well as those of the school to the parents, then the job description would be very different. The home liaison teacher might try to understand the parents' attitude to the school, find ways in which the parents could contribute to the school (the books made by parents in our project were one such example) ask for information about the children which would help the teachers, show the parents how to help the children with whatever skills they were being taught at school, and take up with the school suggestions, problems, and complaints raised by the parents.

An alternative way of organizing this kind of home-school *rapprochement* would be to set up local educational shops or centres. In such a centre the curriculum materials (such as play activities and reading schemes) in the local school could be displayed, the mysteries of school organization and curriculum (like 'blue' and 'red' groups, Fletcher maths, or 'Breakthrough' reading) explained, in a setting where parents might feel more able to ask questions and discuss their anxieties than at an open evening at school. At such a centre it would also be possible for teachers to meet with groups of parents on neutral ground, and specific problems or complaints could be taken up by the organization on behalf of parents.

Professionalism is likely to be a serious obstacle to establishing innovations of this kind. At present teachers are often unwilling to listen to the opinions of parents on educational aims and practices, or to accept that parents can make an important contribution to their child's education, on the grounds that the parents lack the requisite knowledge.

The issue is not a simple one, nor is it unique to the teaching profession. On the one hand professionals *do* have specialized knowledge and skills, which no layman can acquire without himself becoming an expert. When one person has expert knowledge not shared by another, there can be no equality of status in a discussion requiring this knowledge. Most parents in our project were very aware of this fact; either they wished to leave education entirely to the teacher, or they thought that she should be left to make the decisions, after taking into account their opinions and suggestions. They were usually careful to stipulate that any help they offered the teacher, whether in school or at home, should be consistent with her methods.

Unfortunately, professionalism tends to prevent teachers from seeing that within these limits parents have a contribution to make to the school. For example, parents usually have a detailed knowledge of the locality; they may have skills and knowledge which the school could profit from; they may understand better than the teachers the skills their children need to acquire, because of their knowledge of their children and the community in which they live; they may have a point of view on such matters as school rules or hours which should be considered because these issues affect not only the children, but the lives of their families.

Further, professionalism tends to prevent teachers from encouraging parents to help their children with their schooling. It is true that both parents and teachers are uneasy about encroaching on each other's roles, but we found that most parents wanted information about their children's school, and wanted to know how to help them at home. The most frequent parental criticism of the intensive parent involvement programmes set up during the project was that they did not give advice on this matter. In every school, half the parents were trying to teach their under fives to read and write. Middle class parents tended to set about this task with confidence and skill, working class parents with diffidence and anxiety. (Compare the Newsons' evidence on this point, 1977.) There is clearly an enormous additional educational resource here, which could be mobilized by the school. Yet because the teachers disapproved of the parents' concern with formal skills, and considered that teaching children was a professional matter, this resource was not used.

A new definition of professionalism is required to overcome these difficulties. The teacher would expect to use her special skills and knowledge to enlist the help of laymen, she would expect to exchange information with them, and take their opinions into consideration. Such a role would surely enhance, rather than reduce her status.

Many teachers may feel that parental involvement of this kind is likely not only to be threatening, but to involve them in a great deal of work. Yet the notion of 'partnership' with parents, advanced in the Plowden report, can only be given meaning if some measure of consultation and exchange of information with parents is introduced. The advantages for the child of a closer relationship between home and school have always been obvious—at present, the tremendous educational potential of working class parents has hardly been tapped. The experience of our project suggests that there are considerable advantages to the teacher also. If teachers take the trouble repeatedly to explain and discuss their work with parents, they are likely to be rewarded by the support of an interested and appreciative parent body.

There is no question that at the present time some teachers face parents who are far from appreciative and interested. Much can be done within existing educational structures to improve this situation, and in the second part of this book we have a number of detailed suggestions to offer. We have argued, however, that there is a good case for exploring new forms of parental involvement, especially those operating outside the school, which take as a working hypothesis that the school can profit from listening to parents' views, and from developing new ways to draw on their skills, knowledge, and enthusiasm.

8

Policy recommendations

We conclude this section of the book with a brief statement of policy recommendations arising from our study. It should by now be clear that the nature of such recommendations must depend on the reasons for advocating parental involvement. If the aim is no more than to foster friendly staff-parent relationships, a suggestion to increase the number of informal social contacts (social evenings, coffee mornings, staff and family 'fun' outings) may be all that is required. But if, as we believe should be the case, the aim is to increase mutual understanding and support between parents and teachers, and to enlist parents help in the education of their children, then both major changes in teachers' attitudes and extra resources for work with parents are needed. This is because, as explained in the last chapter, in order to achieve these aims teachers require new skills and new attitudes, and they need to be allocated extra time. Many teachers may feel that changes in parental attitudes are also necessary. As we have argued above, we believe that these are only likely to follow sustained attempts by teachers to explain and discuss their work.

Changes in teacher training

1 Changing attitudes

Effective collaboration with parents is not likely to happen unless teachers change their role definition, and broaden their concepts of professionalism; if they are to work with parents, they need to be prepared to consider the parents' points of view, and to respect parents' knowledge of their children, and their potential to help them educationally. Attitude changes of this kind may stem from the experience of collaborating with parents, but initial training courses can also play a part. Tutors can help by extending the student's role definition of a teacher to include work with parents as a recognized part of the job. The importance of spending time with parents can be stressed, as well as the need to give this priority over less important activities. Attitudes to parents can be discussed with students, and the contribution they make to his development can be explained. Colleges should consider encouraging students to spend some time in the children's homes, if they would be welcome, to further this understanding. Students need to become sensitive to cultural differences, and to understand, even if they do not share, parents' attitudes to child-rearing and to education. To further this understanding some of the children's families might be willing to include students in their visits to churches, temples, meeting places, and local shops and markets. To profit from these contacts a student needs to be clear that her goal is not to describe the family's problems or deficits, but to see what she can learn from them, and to relate this to her experiences in school.

If teachers are to enlist the help of parents, and learn from them, they need not only a new role definition, but a new definition of professionalism. This would involve seeing themselves as persons with special skills and knowledge, who are able not only to use those skills with children, but also to explain their work to a lay audience, to acknowledge the educational contribution which parents can make, and to accept that they may have a valid point of view on educational matters. Although at first sight this may seem a lot to ask, it should be remembered that other professionals nowadays do accept the need for this kind of partnership. Doctors, for example, frequently explain their diagnosis and treatment, and enlist the informed cooperation of the patient and his family.

2 Enlarging skills

Even given the will to collaborate with parents, not all teachers know how to set about it effectively. They need certain basic skills for working with parents—such as experience in giving information and explanation about their work both to individual parents and to groups of parents, in running discussion groups with parents, in making home visits, in organizing volunteer help in the classroom, and in explaining to parents how they can help their children at home. Nursery teachers in particular often need help in order to discuss with parents the present functioning of their children in a variety of areas, and the development that can be expected in the next year. Teachers also need to know how to make parent involvement activities interesting, useful and attractive, and how to get feedback on whether these activities are appreciated, and do achieve their goal. If parents don't take part in the activities, they need to form the habit of considering 'What was wrong with the content/timing/organization/publicity of the activity?' before they ask 'What is wrong with the parents?'

Detailed suggestions about organizing such activities are made in the second half of this book. It is unlikely that much time could be made available for this purpose during initial training; further, such work is probably of most profit when teachers can test it out in their own daily experience. For this reason, appropriate in-service courses may be the best medium for giving teachers practical help in organizing and evaluating their work with parents.

Allocation of extra resources

Although, in our opinion, the basic change required is one of attitudes, most additional contacts with parents will encroach on the teacher's time and energy. Some teachers are prepared to do this work in their own time; however, allocating class teachers' time for work with parents, even if only half-a-day a week, not only makes it more feasible, but also legitimizes it. We think that there are many reasons why such a procedure is generally preferable to the appointment of a special home-link or pastoral care teacher (see pages 113–114). However, in areas where there are many minority group parents, a home-liaison teacher from a minority group might take on some of these functions. Other resources, for instance ways of producing attractive communications, are useful, but less crucial than extra teacher time.

Working with minority group parents

There is a great need for more teachers from minority groups. Without such teachers, special efforts and additional resources are needed to enable communication to take place between teachers and minority group parents. In the absence of a shared language, the school needs to ensure that interpreters and translators are available for oral and written communication with the parents; other bilingual parents, or even older children, can be called on for help if necessary. When a school has a large proportion of minority group parents, staff-parent relationships are likely to be improved by staff moves towards the community, as well as by encouraging parents in to the school. For example, school meetings can be held in local temples, or community centres, local community leaders can be invited to schools to talk to staff and children, special efforts can be made to visit families at home. The staff also need to be provided with basic information about the languages, religions, and customs of the individual families they work with. Structured consultations with groups of parents (see below) are particularly necessary in these areas.

Structures for staff-parent discussion

At present many nursery and infant schools have no structures which could be used for an exchange of views between groups of parents and teachers—where PTAs exist, they tend to be vehicles for fund-raising, or organizing talks of a general nature. One way to represent parents' views is *via* parent governors, provided that they organize meetings to solicit parents' views, and report back to them. But especially if there is a marked difference in values and attitudes between parents and staff, opportunities for a more informal exchange of views with a greater proportion of parents are needed. These could be organized at the classroom level, between teachers and parents, or parent representatives from each class could meet with the staff, and perhaps with local community representatives. Whether or not parents are involved in the decision-making processes of the school, structures of this kind would provide opportunities for parent-staff consultation and exchange of views.

Part II

Organizing parent involvement in nursery and infant schools

9

Introduction

In the second part of this book we describe in detail some of the parent involvement activities which took place during the course of our project. Because so many teachers have not received training for this work, we concentrate on practical suggestions for organization, with discussion of possible pitfalls and how to avoid them.

We have prefaced our account of each activity with a discussion of the aims it is intended to fulfil. Any specific involvement activity can be organized in very different ways, depending on the teacher's purpose. For example, 'involving parents in outings' can mean asking them along to help at road junctions, or asking them to help to plan, take part in and evaluate the outing.

In making our suggestions, we have assumed that the teacher's aims in working with parents include keeping them informed, enabling staff and parents to exchange ideas and opinions and to learn from each other, and enabling parents to contribute to the education provided by the school if they wish to do so. Of course, the teacher who reads this book may have much more limited aims—she may simply want parents to give her a helping hand from time to time. For that purpose, she hardly requires our advice, which is addressed to teachers who want to attempt a more difficult and less well charted enterprise.

We have suggested simple methods for evaluating whether

each activity has fulfilled the aims for which it was intended. Any feedback will help the teacher evaluate her success and improve her efforts.

We do not, of course, suggest that any one teacher either could or should organize all the activities we describe. Some activities will be more appropriate for one type of school or area than another—whilst some will appeal to one teacher more than another.

We are *very* aware that there are considerable constraints which limit the amount and kind of parent involvement activity that any particular school can carry out. The class teacher can do very little without a cooperative head. Equally, the head requires teachers who have sufficient confidence to tackle work with parents as well as their ordinary class work. Almost all our suggestions need extra resources of one kind or another, in particular extra help for the teacher to enable her to give time to parents. In each chapter we suggest makeshift ways of organizing extra help. There is no doubt, however, that the most effective parent involvement work calls for a higher level of staffing than is at present available in most schools.

Although our project was carried out in nursery schools and classes, we believe that all the activities can in one way or another be adapted for infant schools. We have included in each chapter suggestions for doing this, based on the experience of our research officers, all of whom were experienced infant teachers.

10

Laying the foundation

Early contacts

Between the day when the parent first contacts the school, and the day on which her child is finally settled into the school routine, is a period when the staff have an opportunity to lay the foundations for successful parental involvement. At this period most parents are very conscious that their child is about to take a significant step, in which he will not only become more independent of them, but also begin his long journey through the educational system. They are often anxious about this step, eager to help him, and keen not to be suddenly excluded from his life. They are likely to be prepared to spend more time in the school than they ever will again, if only because many of them will now go back to work once their children have started full-time school.

Yet though the first contact can be a very positive experience for parents, children and staff, too often this opportunity is not taken up. The parents who come to put a child's name down for admission to the school may go away having done little more than produce the child's birth certificate, and the parent 'settling-in' a child may be left on her own in a corner of the class, uncertain what to do.

The process of 'giving up' a child to the educational system is also likely to induce or confirm parental feelings of inadequacy. Until this time parents have reared their children according to their own standards, with little professional help. Suddenly, 'experts' take over the education of the child; the parents' own knowledge and experience of him appears to be no longer valued. In consequence they may see education as something to be left to the school. If teachers seek parents' cooperation, they need from the start to show that they value their help.

Aims of first contacts with parents

● To make the child's transition to school as easy and pleasant as possible

● To show parents that they are welcome in the school, and can feel comfortable there

● To explain the school's aims and methods to the parents

● To provide the staff with opportunities to learn from the parents about their child

The first contact with the school

When the parent brings a child to put his name down for admission, the first step in welcoming them both into the life of the school can be taken. They should be shown around the school, introduced to any staff they meet, taken to the nursery or reception class, and invited to stay there for a while. While they are in the class they should not be left too long to their own devices—one of the staff or another parent needs to talk to them about the daily routine, how the equipment is used, and so on, otherwise both parent and child are likely to feel awkward. They should be shown the cloakroom, toilets, playground, and dining hall as well as the classroom, so that they can prepare their child by talking to him about the new experiences he will have. Before they leave the school, they should be given a copy of the school prospectus, and the pending home visit should be mentioned. If a home visit is not to be made, some of the matters which would be discussed then should be raised, or the parent could be invited to return on another occasion for such a discussion. Finally, the parent and child should be invited to visit school as often as possible in the period before the child is due to start. Where the parents do not speak English the priority will be to arrange for an interpreter as soon as possible to enable 'first contact' plans to be explained to the parents.

Visiting school before the child is officially admitted

Starting school can be a less painful process than it sometimes is if the child gradually gets to know the staff and the class *before* the term in which he is due to start. There are a number of different ways in which this can be done, depending on the size and layout of the school, and the staff available. If space is available, it may be possible to organize a 'preschool club' once or twice a week (see pages 136–40). If the nursery or reception class is big enough, parents could be invited to call in with their child and spend a little while in the class whenever they are passing the school. It might be possible to arrange one area of the room for this purpose, with adult sized chairs and suitable toys. On such occasions, it's important that the teacher or her assistant talks to the mother and child, and suggests what they might do while in the class. Many parents in our project told us how uneasy they felt in a classroom when nobody spoke to them. If neither of these arrangements is possible, the school might have a 'drop in' area for parents, with a kettle, comfortable chairs and a few toys and books, either in the entrance hall or in a special parents' room. Here parents and children can get to know each other, but they will also need to be invited into the classroom sometimes so that the children will become familiar with it.

Whatever the arrangement, the aim should be to encourage parents and the children due to start school to call in quite frequently, meet other mothers and preschool children, and get to know the staff, the buildings, and the way the school functions.

Home visiting before the child starts school

Home visits offer an opportunity for the teacher, the child and his parents to get to know each other away from the atmosphere of the school. There is no doubt that most parents *do* find school intimidating; in their own home, where they are host, they can be more relaxed, more forthcoming with questions, opinions, and information. They are also better able to see the teacher as a person when she is out of school, and their appreciation of the time and attention being given to them forms a basis for a positive relationship.

Equally, the teacher benefits by getting a fuller picture of the child's out-of-school life, which will help her to develop a relationship with him at school. She also has the opportunity to explain in full her educational aims, what she is trying to achieve with the children, and how she works.

We ourselves were very impressed by the effect home visiting had on our own relationships with the families in our project. At the start of the project we interviewed all the families at home, and usually stayed on chatting after the interview was complete. This informal contact at home made it very easy to relate to both children and parents when we later met them at school. We do not think that home visits should be regarded as a way of finding out about a family's 'problems'—teachers are not social workers. The visits should rather be seen as an opportunity for gaining and giving useful positive information, and laying the basis of a friendly relationship between teacher, parent and child.

Wasted journeys can be avoided by making an appointment for the visit by letter or telephone, or in person when the parent registers the child.

How can time for home-visiting be found? Ideally, extra staff are needed to allow all class teachers time to visit parents. In our project some teachers visited during school hours, others during the evening. Visits can be made during school hours if the head or an assistant, perhaps helped by one or two parents, will take over the class in the teacher's absence. In some reception classes children attend only part-time until they are five. This can mean that the teacher has few or even no children for part of the day. In these circumstances when she is free she tends to be used as a remedial or 'floating' teacher, but her time could be used instead for home visits.

But teachers may *not* be able to leave school in the day, and working mothers may not be home to be visited. Some teachers in our project thought it worthwhile to make after-school evening visits in their own time. After all, most teachers maintain that their working-day does not end at 3.30—home visits can be seen as equivalent to other after school activities, such as preparing materials. Obviously, a car or a bicycle is a great help, and may make an occasional home visit during the lunch hour possible, if this time is convenient for the parent.

We have found that teachers can be very nervous of home visiting, fearing perhaps that they will be seen as interfering busy-bodies, that they will be faced with hostility or in some way find themselves unable to cope. However, in our project, of the four teachers who did home visits, none ever received a hostile reception. And, in answering our questionnaires, parents had only appreciative comments to make about home visits.

It may be necessary for the teacher to start by explaining that she would like to come in for a chat, since some parents may be uncertain as to whether she wants to be invited into the house. Often it helps to take a list of the points to cover in the interview. This should include important information to help the teacher relate to the child—such as the names and ages of his brothers and sisters, the names of other significant people in his life, and his pets, the extent to which he has left home before, what sort of things he likes doing. It is useful to ask whether the child can manage going to the lavatory on his own, to tell the family about the daily routine of the class, and the name of the nursery or welfare assistant, and perhaps to show the family photos of the class, and encourage them to raise any questions that they may have.

The teacher can also discuss the best way to prepare the child for school—many parents still feel that the child should be threatened or warned to be on his best behaviour. She may wish to recommend books and toys that he might particularly enjoy. We do not think it is useful to suggest to parents that the child should have achieved certain goals before starting school—for instance tying his shoe laces—unless the teacher is prepared to spend time explaining and demonstrating how this can be done. Even then, the idea of a deadline to be met can be alarming. However, the teacher could suggest that parents encourage their children to do as much for themselves as possible.

The visit is also a golden opportunity to explain ways in which the parents can be involved in the work of the class and school and discuss with them whether they have any special skills, hobbies or interests which they can, and would like to, contribute.

When the family is from a minority group it is important to obtain information about what languages are spoken at home, and what religious and cultural customs and activities the child is involved in. It will be helpful to discuss with the parents how these could be incorporated into the child's life at school. It may also be necessary to discuss arrangements for an interpreter to be available on a regular basis when the child starts school.

Some of the teachers in our project became so convinced of the value of home visits that they found time for them on other occasions, such as during the term before a child's transfer to infant school, or when a child was ill. Most of the parents would have welcomed additional home visits, because of the opportunity they offer for private discussion on the parents' own ground. We suspect that home visiting is only unpopular with parents when it seems that the purpose of the visit is to complain about a child, or to investigate family problems and circumstances. A visit with clearly defined aims, in which the teacher hopes to learn from the parent and exchange information with her, is very different in character.

There is no doubt that home visiting is time consuming, and can generally not be carried out without extra staff. Some schools appoint special 'community' or 'pastoral' teachers for this work, but we think it is important that the class teacher should do her own home visiting. It is only the class teacher who knows the child well enough to discuss his work or behaviour in detail, and equally it is the teacher who actually works with the child who needs to be helped by information from the parents, and an improved relationship with them. All but one of the staff in our project would have liked to use extra staff to free themselves for home visits on say, one half-day a week, or to be given time off during the day in lieu of time spent visiting in the evening. There may also be a case for an educational visitor as a neutral mediator between home and school (see pages 113–14), but her home visits would fulfil a rather different function.

Contacts in the term before the child starts school

By this time the parents and child should be used to 'dropping in' to school. It would now be helpful to encourage parents to spend occasional regular sessions in the class with their child. If the child is to start full-time school, visits should if possible, include playtime and lunchtime, since these are times when children may not be with their familiar teacher or nursery nurse and have a host of new faces and noise, the lavatories and the cloakroom to cope with. Even children attending the school's 'preschool club' (see pages 136–40) would be helped by the opportunity to spend a whole session in their future classroom.

These visits may be best arranged by inviting a few parents and children at a time and organizing the session so that a member of staff or an 'old' parent is free to talk to them for part of the time. Established parents can be very helpful here—they can talk about their own experiences when their children started school, introduce new parents to others, and so forth. In a reception class this may be harder to organize, but a series of mornings or afternoons could be set aside when groups of new parents and children could be invited and the class programme altered to accommodate visitors.

A slightly different purpose would be served by one or two informal evening meetings, to which parents, particularly fathers and working mothers, could go without their children. These meetings could be used as an opportunity for parents and staff to meet informally, and talk about their children's feelings about starting school, how they have responded to stories/talk/play about school, how they have reacted to their visits to school, and so on. They can talk about what they have seen on their visits to the class and the teacher can use the time to explain her aims and methods. Parents whose children started earlier in the year and who probably had many of the same questions and feelings could also be invited to share their experiences with 'new' parents.

Settling into school

By the time the child finally starts school he should already be familiar with the classroom, staff, class routine, and if possible some of the other children. The widespread current practice of admitting children gradually at the beginning of term will give staff time to renew their relationship with individual children, already started on the basis of a home visit, and earlier visits by the children to school.

If the gradual 'getting used to school' policy described above has been followed, many children will now leave their parents without much difficulty. In many schools the nursery teacher asks the mother to stay for the first few sessions. In some cases this may be very difficult—working mothers may have to lose money they cannot afford, others may be ill. Sometimes a relative or friend can help in these instances, but if this is not possible mothers whose children are already in the class, or whose children have moved up, may be able to help in the class in order to give the staff more time to devote to an unhappy child.

In our project we found that both teachers and mothers were often uneasy during the settling in period. The teacher might feel the mother should be left to settle her child on her own, yet the mother might not know how to do this, and feel embarrassed or distressed because her child was clinging and unhappy. It seems to work best if the staff try to develop a relationship with the child and involve him in activities with them, while 'established' parents talk to new parents.

If the child takes a long time to settle, his parents could be asked to help the staff, for instance by reading stories to small groups of children, or helping with the various activities. This strategy both makes them feel useful, and helps them to get to know some of the other children.

The impression the teacher gives to parents at this early stage is important. The parent needs to feel confident that her child will not be allowed to cry for long, and that she will be consulted if the teacher has any problems with him. It helps if the teacher can say something positive about each child when the parents come to collect them, because most parents are anxious to know how their child has 'behaved' at school.

Evaluations

● Keep records of home visits. At the end of the first term, decide whether the right topics were covered in the visits.

● Keep records of visits to the class by future pupils. Families who make no visits may be encouraged by a written invitation or another home visit, but if mothers are working it may be necessary to organize an evening meeting for them.

● Towards the end of the year, ask the mothers for their views
on the settling in process, either through a discussion group or
by using a suggestion box. Could it have been made easier for
them and their children in any way? Can they suggest improvements, or additional information they would have liked to
receive?

Preschool clubs

In the previous section we argued that the period *before* the child
starts school is a key time in which to establish contacts with
parents, and make a gradual transition between home and
school. One way to do this is to start a 'preschool club' for
children due to start school next year. A preschool club is not
intended to be an alternative to an ordinary playgroup or
mother and toddler club, which many of the children may
already be attending. It is rather an additional service for all
children, even those already attending playgroups, to help them
and their parents gradually to get used to the school staff and
environment, and to meet other parents and children in the year
before they start at school. It could usefully be incorporated into
both nursery and infant schools.

Parents can be invited to the club when they come to register
their child. Parents already on the waiting list can be reminded
of it if they are visited at home. In order to reach those families
who are eligible but who are not known to the school, posters
can be displayed in various parts of the catchment area, such as
the clinic, the launderette, or the library. They may need to be
translated into the languages of people in the local community.
The local teachers' centre or community centre may be able to
help with this, or other parents may interpret or translate. If
there is a home tutoring scheme for English as a Foreign
Language in the local education authority, the staff may be
able to tell local parents about the club, or bring them along
to it.

Organizing, staffing, and equipping the club

Ideally, for the preschool club to enable children to develop friendly relationships, and for the parents to become truly involved, frequent attendance is best. But the decision as to how often the group will meet will depend on other factors.

If the club will be meeting in the nursery or reception class, then it is probably only feasible to set it up once or twice a week perhaps in the lunch hour. In a really large reception class, or in a spacious open-plan nursery school, the preschool club might be held in one corner of the area while it is in session and hence could meet more often. A special area could be arranged with adult-sized chairs for mothers. The younger children will gradually venture out in to the other parts of the room, and mix with the older children.

Another possible site for the club in an infant school is the school hall, which is likely to be available at certain times in the week. Using the hall has the advantage that if the nursery or reception class hold group activities in it during part of the 'club time', the staff can encourage mothers and children to join in some of the games, singing or story times. With falling school rolls some schools have spare rooms, or a parents' room, and if one of these is to be used for the club, then meetings could be more frequent. The advantage of using a spare room is that mothers can chat and babies can make a noise in it without disturbing the class. The disadvantage is that unless efforts are made to ensure that the staff are free to spend some time with the group, mothers may feel isolated, and some of the aims of the club will not be fulfilled.

If the locality is well served by playgroups, or if many mothers are working, few parents are likely to want to attend frequently. The main aim of the teacher will then be to encourage all parents to try to bring their children to the club occasionally; a club attendance of six parents with their children is likely to be enjoyable for the families without putting too much strain on the resources of the school.

Organizing parent involvement

Who would staff the preschool club?

The nursery or reception class teacher has a limited amount of time and energy, as well as a commitment to the children in her class. But parents, either of the established class or of the preschool children, can play a large part in organizing and running the club. The teacher should arrange to be present at certain times so that the important goal of establishing relations between staff and parents may be achieved. Perhaps a committee of parents and staff could be formed to carry out the planning.

The teacher's role, once the group is set up, is to make the parents and children feel welcome and at ease in the school, to get to know the parents and children, to help in planning club activities and to help to involve the parents further in the education of their children by discussion and by drawing them into school activities.

If the school has a nursery class, equipment for the preschool group can perhaps be borrowed. If the school has no nursery other possibilities must be explored; the local education authority or social services department may make a grant, parents in the school may donate their children's outgrown toys, parents may be able to raise money, for instance by running a 'thrift shop'.* Wherever the equipment comes from, a decision will be necessary about where it will be kept, and who will be responsible for checking that it is returned or put away after use, and is kept in good order.

What to do in the preschool club

Unlike the playgroup, where the parent leaves her child for the session, the aims of the preschool club involve the parent

* A fund-raising activity, when parents bring goods to sell to other parents, perhaps once a week or once a month, keeping a proportion of the sums raised for themselves.

staying—helping to organize it, and talking to the staff. The question of insurance and legal responsibility would have to be taken up with the local education authority. The parent does not need to be at her child's side all the time—she may be taking part in a discussion in another room, but she should be available if needed, and responsible for her child. Many of the families will bring along younger children who will have to be catered for. Very young babies are little trouble, they will sleep or play in their prams and all that is required is somewhere in the class or corridor to leave the prams. Babies able to crawl, and toddlers, will need suitable play equipment.

If plenty of play material and tea and coffee are available, parents and children can simply enjoy each other's company. But it is important that the staff who will be working with the children next year should spend some time in the club each week. As well as getting to know the children, they can explain to the parents why certain kinds of play material are provided, and discuss books and toys with them. The parents and children could join in school occasions such as harvest festival, Christmas celebrations, perhaps occasional assemblies, which would increase their feeling of being involved in the children's school.

Once the children are confident enough to play together and leave their parents' side, and the parents have got to know each other a little, they might like to form a discussion group for the exchange of ideas and information. Information in the form of leaflets, posters, booklets, from the education or social services department, the Health Education Council, Gingerbread, the Commission for Racial Equality, and so on, could be made available, and health visitors and welfare rights workers could come along to talk to the group. There could be leaflets on local places to visit with children, with details of how to get there, the cost, and what to do there. Parents may be interested in learning more about child development or specific skills, in which case the staff may be able to provide workshop sessions on, for example, pre-reading and pre-writing activities or tell them about a prepared course which the group could follow, such as the Open University Courses 'The First Years of Life' or 'The Preschool Years'.

Discussion groups of this kind are only likely to develop among regular club attenders, and they would require extra help—someone to look after the club children while the parents met, or someone to help in the nursery or reception classroom whilst the teachers talked with the parents. It is possible that another parent (perhaps from a local preschool playgroup), the head teacher, a welfare assistant, or a student would help on these occasions. As with most of our suggestions, however, it is clear that extra activities require extra resources.

Working mothers may find it difficult or impossible to attend the club. The more frequent the meetings and the more flexible the time (in the mornings on some days, and in the afternoons on others) the easier it will be for some working mothers to attend. Efforts should be made to encourage whoever is caring for the children of those parents who work full time to bring them along, so that the children get some benefit from the club before they start school. Contacts could be made with local playgroups, day nurseries and childminders. There may be childminders among the mothers who would welcome the opportunity not only to bring the children in their care to play with other children and toys, but to meet other mothers.

Evaluation

● Keep a note of who comes and how often, so as to know which 'prospective' parents need to be contacted by other methods.
● After half a term or at the end of the term, ask the parents for their views, anything they particularly like or dislike about the club, whether the time and place are the most convenient, whether they have any suggestions to make. Parents may be unwilling to make criticisms directly so a suggestion box or a large poster on the wall where they could tick a list of positive or negative comments might be helpful.

11

Giving parents information

A school prospectus

Many new parents know little or nothing about their children's schools, and a written prospectus is one way of informing them. It has the advantage that parents can study the information in a leisurely way at home, show it to their friends and relatives, and keep it to refer to later. The prospectus should give information that is useful in helping parents understand the work of the school and in indicating how they can be involved. Whatever form the prospectus takes it should be attractively produced and written in a style that is readable. All technical and specialized language should be avoided.

Contents

Every school is different so we can do no more than point out the questions we found that parents wanted to have answered, and the topics that can be usefully covered. The best way to decide what should go in a prospectus is to ask present parents what they would have liked to have been told before their children started at the school, and discuss with all staff what they would like to tell parents. Parents at our project schools made many useful suggestions, and discussions with them were particularly important in schools where there were parents who had not themselves attended school in the United Kingdom. In such schools it may be welcoming or even necessary to offer translations of the prospectus in one or more languages, and also to include a description of the place of the school within the education system. This would be easier to arrange if there were parent groups representing the different minority groups in the school (see page 221). A nursery school, for example, might explain that it 'feeds' several primary schools, and that reading and writing are taught in the infant, rather than the nursery school.

Parents need brief information about the staff and pupils—the names of the teachers, their qualifications and special responsibilities, which classes they teach; the usual number of pupils on roll, the size of classes, age groupings, how children move up, how children are grouped into classes. The names and responsibilities of all ancillary staff should also be included.

Parents can be told about the role they can play in all aspects of school life. Well chosen examples will give them a clearer idea of the school's expectations and willingness to involve all parents. They also need information about the parent teacher association, its function and activities, and information about facilities for parents in the school—such as notice boards, or the parents' room.

Parents will want to know how they can find out what their child is doing at school and what means are provided for them to participate in decisions about this. A comprehensive list would be best here, including arrangements for talking to the head and teachers: when they are available, how to make an appointment.

The following are suggestions for parent involvement which could be included in a prospectus.

'How you can be involved in our school'

● Visit the class. Each class has a time for parents to watch or join in.

- Come to our parents' meetings.

- Make an appointment to talk to the teacher. Teachers may be able to visit you at home if you can't get to the school.

- Look at your child's work whenever you come to school.

- Watch for displays of work in corridors, hall, classes and foyer.

- Talk to other parents about their children's work. Find out what they think of what's going on.

- If you have a complaint, worry, or problem about something to do with school do let us know; or tell the parent governors who will take it up.

- Talk to the parent governors—their job is to know what's happening and what is going to happen in the school.

- Come to our assemblies. It's a good time to find out about what's going on in other classes.

- Come and work with us. (Talk to the class teacher about what you would like to do.)

- Visit other schools and see what's happening there. This will help you see what's possible, and you will be able to bring new ideas to our school.

- Meetings of the Council are open to the public. You may like to go to an Education Committee meeting where the decisions affecting all schools in the authority are made.

- Find out what your child will be doing at her next school. Ask neighbours, visit the school and then discuss it with us.

Parents are often mystified by vague phrases in a prospectus such as 'We aim to help all our children reach their full potential.' They will get a better picture of what their childen will be doing if the activities and subjects offered are listed, including names of reading, maths and other schemes used. A brief account of how children and work are organized, how decisions are made about what individual children do, and when reports, records of work, etc, are available for parents should be included.

Parents will want to know how often the children do physical education and games, what games are played and where, and whether special clothing is required for physical education.

We found many parents were concerned about safety procedures at school. The prospectus could include reassuring details such as the frequency of fire drills, the procedure followed if a child has an accident or is ill, the responsibility of the welfare assistant for dispensing medicine and first aid, who takes responsibility for children after school and on outings.

Parents also like to know about the arrangements made at dinner time—who supervises the children, whether children are made to eat everything, where the menu can be seen, the cost of meals and how to obtain free meals, arrangements for special diets.

Brief information about the school medical service, dental inspections and the work of the school nurse should also be included—for instance when children are examined, whether parents should be present, how they are kept informed of the results of inspections.

If parents are to be fully involved in the life of the school, their views heard and their support called on, they are entitled to have full information about the running of the school—who is responsible for the school, who administers it, what are the sources of finance, and so forth. This information can be given under such headings as:

The Local Education Authority—its responsibilities and powers

The Governing Body—the governors and their relation to the LEA; how they are selected; what they do; their responsibilities; how to get something discussed at governors' meetings; the role of parent governors; how to set about becoming a school governor

Notes on producing and distributing the prospectus

An interesting cover, for example one with a photograph, will go a long way to making the prospectus look attractive. If this is too expensive, children's drawings are an appealing alternative. We found that the usual resources of nursery and infant schools—Banda or Roneo duplicators—were not really adequate to produce an attractive prospectus. Local secondary schools may be able to help. They usually have better reprographic facilities than nursery or infant schools. Alternative sources of help would be teachers' centres, and other educational establishments such as colleges of education, art or technical colleges. The cost of producing a prospectus with a professional finish depends very much on the format and on the number printed at any one time. We found that some printers were prepared to print at a discount when convinced they were providing a community service.

Costs can be reduced by organizing pages or sections so that some parts can be altered without the need to reprint the whole booklet. It also saves reprinting costs if spaces can be left in the text to be filled in by hand, for instance staff names, and pupil names. Most schools will have little difficulty in finding or raising funds to cover the cost of producing the prospectus, which should be supplied free to all parents.

The kind of prospectus we have described could be interesting to a wider audience than new and prospective parents. Schools who want to build links with the local community might consider making it available in public places, such as the local clinics, children's libraries, or doctors' waiting rooms. Health visitors, social and community workers, and local community centres and churches might also like a copy.

Organizing parent involvement

Evaluation

● Ask parents at the end of their first year in school how helpful they found the prospectus, and whether they can suggest additions or deletions.

Newsletters and noticeboards

Written notes and letters are the main form of communication between school and home in the primary school. They are sometimes ineffective, patronizing, illegible, or incomprehensible. Parents often seem irritated by the remorseless succession of letters brought home—or lost—by their children, and they may ignore the contents.

It is worth considering why parents groan when their child produces a letter from school. Often the appearance of the letter is unprepossessing and the contents are concerned with trying to involve the parent in some unappealing activity, such as fund-raising or attending a potentially boring school meeting. In our project we helped teachers to produce class newsletters, containing information which we knew from our interviews that parents would be interested in receiving. Of course, some parents will scarcely glance at any letter, however attractive, and will prefer to spend time talking to the teacher; a few may be illiterate. But we found that most parents appreciated the opportunity to read the newsletters at leisure in their homes, and found the information included of value.

Class newsletters

The class newsletter, besides giving essential administrative information about dates of terms and meetings, should include information about the work of the class; suggestions for home activities related to work being done in the class; copies of songs

146

and rhymes the children are learning; suggestions for weekend and holiday activities; requests for suggestions and help. In infant schools newsletters could contain, in addition, details of new schemes of work being introduced and of new books or apparatus acquired, and information about activities parents may rarely see, like PE or music. This kind of information helps parents to make more sense of what their children tell them, and to feel in touch with the class activities. The newsletter could also include a 'post bag' from parents, with letters, comments and suggestions. A small ads column, for buying and selling and advertising local events, will increase its interest.

The frequency with which these letters are produced will depend on the enthusiasm of the teacher and the help she gets. Some parents may be willing to give very extensive help, or even to edit and produce the newsletter, after discussing with the teacher what she would like included, and asking her for copies of the information required. A class 'sign' will help to distinguish the newsletter from all the other school missives, and older children might help with drawings.

Evaluation

● Once parents have received two or three newsletters, try to ask every parent what they think of them, either personally or through the next newsletter. Ask for suggestions for improving them, and for other topics that parents would like included. Continue to canvass opinion once a term.

Class noticeboards

Where the majority of parents bring their children to school themselves notices on a noticeboard fixed in a prominent position can serve many of the same purposes as newsletters. They have the advantage of not requiring duplication. In addition, general information about the class can be displayed, such as names of staff with photographs; notes about the class routine and organization; names of the children in each class; menus, and so on. In our project, one teacher put up her plans for activities each week with explanations of the purpose of the activity. Another used an easel placed alongside the classroom door at going home time to give one or two items of day-to-day news about the nursery class. With older children similar news items could be written by the children themselves.

All such news items need to be regularly changed and consistently displayed. We found that at first it was necessary to draw parents' attention to the board, but later it became a habit for most parents to have a look at it each day. Some parents welcomed a space on the board for their own use—to advertise goods for sale and local events they were involved in. This will inevitably increase interest in looking at the noticeboard. Both newsletters and notices should be easy and quick to read and well produced. Notices should be eyecatching, and brief, and it is a good idea to have a special place on the board for news.

Translations

All letters should ideally be written in the language of the home. Notices should be translated where there is a sizeable minority language group. However, if there are only one or two parents speaking a minority language and translation facilities are poor, or if some parents are illiterate, other means of communication—home visits, personal chats, regular meetings with an interpreter will have to be used with them.

Evaluation

● When the class noticeboard has been up for a month, try to find out whether parents are actually using it. Do they discuss what they've read or even read it? A notice could be on the board asking parents to tick when they've read it, explaining that you want to find out how many parents are looking at the notice-board, and whether it is fulfilling a useful function.

Parents' meetings

Most schools hold meetings for parents, but often only a minor-ity attend, and even fewer participate in discussion. Many teachers complain that the parents they would like to see never come. One useful approach to this problem is to consider whether there is something wrong with the meetings rather than the parents. Why don't parents attend school meetings?

For many people, going out to a meeting, especially in the evening, is an effort. For those who have just returned home from work even greater effort is required to turn out again, especially in cold wet weather. The meeting has also to compete with favourite TV programmes and family routines. All of this adds up to the fact that a school is unlikely to get a majority of parents to its meetings unless they think it will be of value to them, interesting, and enjoyable.

Many of the parents we interviewed who had never attended a meeting at school before the start of our project indicated that they did not give high priority to such events—it wasn't worth the effort; but at the same time they were all keen to know more about their children's work and progress at school. Other reasons they gave for not attending were that they did not have a babysitter, that the meetings were at an inconvenient time, or that they were uneasy about going alone.

The meetings we subsequently organized attempted to take all these factors into account. Possible topics for meetings were discussed with parents, all parents were asked which days and times they preferred, a crèche was provided at evening meet-ings, and parents who would have to come alone were en-couraged to bring a friend or relative. At the meetings we often showed films or slides of the children in the class, or held workshops, where parents could examine and try out the children's equipment and materials.

Organizing parent involvement

We found that the topics parents were most interested in were those specifically related to their own children's education—such as early reading, early maths, writing, how to help their children at home, the transition to infant school. Attendance at these meetings was very high—from 75 to 95 per cent of families were represented. Meetings with outside speakers and commercial films, and talks on general subjects like 'the importance of play' were less popular, as they were not usually seen as directly relevant by the parents.

Aims of meetings

- Giving and receiving information
- Exchanging ideas and opinions
- Airing problems and complaints
- Developing closer social relationships

Types of meeting

No single type of meeting will be able to fulfil all these aims effectively. Gathering a large group of parents together has the advantage for the teacher that she can give information to many people in a short time. The disadvantages are the limited amount of discussion that can take place in a large meeting, and the fact that most people will not speak their minds in a large group, or get to know other parents. We found that holding meetings for the parents of one class only had advantages—the parents had more in common and were more likely to know each other. There is much to be said for even smaller meetings with about 8–12 parents. These might take the form of coffee mornings, mothers' clubs or workshops. Potentially, a small meeting of this kind can be more effective than any other.

When the same group meets regularly, parents and teachers can get to know each other better and can discuss matters freely and in more detail. Purely social evenings are usually popular with parents, and the closer relationships between parents and between parents and staff which may develop help to make later discussion easier.

When and where to have meetings

It is never possible to arrange a time to suit everyone but consulting with parents first will increase the possibility of choosing a time convenient for the majority. We found in some schools it was necessary to repeat meetings to accommodate the needs of shift workers. It may be that for some schools Sunday is a better day than a weekday, or that starting at 8.30 p.m. may be preferable to 7.30 p.m., when some people have only just returned from work.

If there are a number of parents who do not go out to work and who bring their children to school a meeting can be held in school hours, for instance at the beginning or towards the end of the day. We found this a good time to hold regular small group meetings like coffee mornings, and workshops. A box of toys and biscuits and drinks need to be provided for toddlers who accompany their parents. This arrangement is, of course, only possible if help is available to look after the class—for example an assistant aided by a student or parent, or the head teacher, if she will help out.

Where should meetings be held?

Many people find schools very uncongenial places in which to spend an evening. They have the feeling of 'being sent to the head master' whenever they enter a school building, despite the friendliness of the staff, or the changes made since they were at school. It is worth considering holding meetings in other local premises—a community centre, a clubhouse, institute, or religious meeting place, a room above a pub, or a parent's home. These will often have other advantages apart from being non-school. They may have other rooms available for a crèche, or a bar, better cloakroom and lavatories, and adult size furniture, and parents will probably feel more relaxed in these surroundings. The disadvantages of holding meetings outside school are that the equipment and materials needed may not be available and parents will not overcome their feeling of anxiety when they do enter the school. A successful pleasant time spent in school can help dispel such anxieties.

Invitations, reminders and summaries

The best method of inviting parents to a meeting is to ask them personally to come, telling them what it's about and saying why you think it's important and worth the effort. Most infants teachers see fewer parents than nursery teachers do, so personal invitations are more difficult, and may involve an hour or so calling on parents at home. We found that this personal touch paid off and the time spent was well worth while.

It is a good idea also to give every parent a letter or card with clear information—as well as the date, time and venue, the details of the programme, and childminding facilities. The length of time the meeting is likely to last should also be included. We found parents were more willing to attend when they had a clear idea of what was involved. These letters, as well as any posters, need to be written in the languages known to the parents. Often, a bilingual parent will help with this task. Posters can be displayed to serve as reminders and to encourage interest. Where large groups of parents are invited it is worth considering displaying them in local shops.

We found that most parents need reminders during the week of the meeting, and also the day before. Children can do this, reminder slips can be sent home, any parent seen at school can be reminded in person, posters can have a band stuck across them saying 'Tomorrow'. The telephone can also be used for jogging parents' memories. If the meeting is to be a small one, parents who have been involved in planning and organizing the meeting are likely to help by encouraging and generating interest among other parents.

One teacher in our project arranged for two of the parents to make notes, and then to write a summary of what happened at her meetings, the topics discussed, and the points made. This was then circulated to all parents who didn't attend. This service was much appreciated.

Interpreters

The provision of interpreters where necessary at meetings is discussed on pages 237–8.

Child-care arrangements for meetings

An important reason why some parents don't attend meetings is that they have no-one with whom they can leave their children. They may not be in the habit of using babysitters, or they may not be able to afford to pay them. This need present no problems for small day-time meetings and discussion groups if a reasonably large room is available. The staff can make it clear that babies and young children are welcome, and suitable toys can be provided in a corner of the room, so that toddlers can see their mothers and can be seen. The meeting is likely to be noisy, but parents are used to making themselves heard over the noise of children.

Evening meetings present greater problems. Older children must be provided for, and younger children may be tired and fractious. One answer is to organize a crèche.

We found that when a crèche was provided at meetings, over half the parents used it. It must provide for all the children of parents attending, not just the children who attend the school. Our crèches catered for babies and children up to 13, though most parents made other arrangements for their older children.

There is no doubt that running a crèche involves a lot of organization, and not all teachers will find it feasible. But it may be the only way in which a single parent, or both parents, can attend evening meetings. Even so, there are special problems in looking after the under threes (see page 155) and not all parents will want to leave their children with strangers.

In order to staff the crèche, other teachers, assistants or students can be called on. It is a good idea to arrange a rota so that they can attend part of the meeting. It may be possible to give crèche staff time off during the day in return. Students on teaching practice or secondary school students, who already help in the class, may be available for help. It is essential to find out how many children will be in the crèche in order to arrange staffing numbers. A minimum of one adult to 10 children is needed for school age children, but if younger children come a higher ratio will be needed.

We found that children of seven upwards were usually content to watch television and play card and board games or look at comics, with little supervision. With luck, babies will sleep in their prams. Children of an intermediate age need more organizing and adult attention. Television, drawing and colouring and the usual 'table toys' should be provided, interspersed with stories and singing. Providing a drink and biscuits helps to break up the time. We found that the crèches worked best if the time was limited to about two hours. Younger children became very tired and fractious after this. This should be borne in mind when planning the meeting.

How much space is needed depends on the numbers of children and adults. The children will be easier to mind if they are in small groups, so if several rooms are available and there is staff to man them it is a good idea to make use of those rooms.

The rooms chosen should also be near to the lavatories, if possible.

Crèche arrangements should be explained beforehand to all parents and children. Parents should be asked to make clear to their children in advance that they will be in another room, not with them. Where there is a large number of children using the crèche it may be necessary to have parents sign their names, both on bringing and on retrieving their children, and to label children if staff don't know them.

The problem of very young children at evening meetings

Easiest to mind are the babies in prams—they usually sleep. The most difficult are very young children from about 12 months to three years. Older brothers and sisters can sometimes be persuaded to entertain them for brief periods, and it is helpful to have a few special toys to bring out when interest wanes. Most of these children need their own personal minder who is able to give them undivided attention for much of the time. Even so, they may be unhappy with strangers. If it is not possible to have a high staff ratio it is advisable to explain the difficulties beforehand to parents and ask them to make other arrangements for very young children if at all possible, or bring an older child to keep the toddler company in the crèche.

Evaluation

● Find out who didn't come and why, in order to decide if it's necessary to change the time of, or the contents of the meeting. To this end the names of everyone at the meeting can be listed, or parents can be asked to sign their names. It is important to explain the reason for this to parents, so that they don't think they are being harassed.

● The success of the meeting can be assessed by trying to find out what the parents who did come thought of it, whether they found out anything new, and what they particularly enjoyed and disliked. Parents can be asked personally for their opinions. Small meetings can be evaluated by discussion amongst those present.

● Ask for suggestion for future meetings.

Making films for and with parents

A film about the class is a guaranteed way of attracting parents to school. In our project we found that between 75 and 100 per cent of families would come to film meetings, provided that they were offered at least two different opportunities to attend. Not only did the parents come, but they were very enthusiastic about the films. Fathers and working mothers, who rarely if ever have the chance to watch their children in school, were particularly appreciative. But all the parents enjoyed being able to watch the children without the feeling that their presence was a distraction.

Films have other advantages. On film you can follow a child through all the aspects of a school day, which few if any parents could manage by visiting the school. You can make a record of a school outing or journey, so that parents can to some extent share the experience. You can also focus on a particular activity, such as mathematics work in the class, and demonstrate the steps in the teaching process and the variety of activities involved. By making a film in stages you can show how children develop during the course of a year. Films can often be a very effective stimulus to discussion: when some aspect of school life is presented vividly and concretely parents and staff may feel more confident to discuss it than if the issue is raised in an abstract way.

In schools where there are parents who do not speak English, films can be particularly helpful. If the films are planned with care a great deal of information can be portrayed visually, with no need for a commentary. It is also possible to show the film and use an interpreter afterwards to answer any questions. Finally, films can be an effective means for parents to contribute to the school life. By making films about the children's lives out of school, and about the neighbourhood, they can produce valuable material for parents, staff and children to discuss. Teachers in multi-racial schools will find such contributions especially helpful.

Aims

● To enable parents, especially those who can't visit the school during the day, to see the children's life at school

● To enable the teacher to explain her teaching methods, and demonstrate the progress of the children, in a vivid and appealing way

● To stimulate discussion about the curriculum and school activities

● To stimulate discussion about children's out-of-school lives, at home and in their local community

Video recordings or cine-films?

Video sets work like ordinary tape recorders, but record pictures as well as sound. To show the film you connect the recorder to a television set. The sets may not need to be specially adapted to accept a video signal: for example the Decca monitor in many schools needs no modification. The new video cassette recorders also only require a standard television set.

Video recording has several advantages over cine-films. If you own or can borrow the equipment, the tapes are fairly cheap and you can use the same tape several times. After recording you can immediately rewind the tape and watch what you have just filmed on the television or, with portable equipment, on the tiny monitor screen in the camera. Although you need to plan your recording, if you are dissatisfied you can start again and film over the tape. The video tape can be 'edited' by this method of re-recording. Another advantage is that when showing a video recording it is possible to stop the film at any time and hold the picture still. This can help when clarifying particular points.

A portable tape deck can be carried around on a shoulder strap. The camera can be hand-held, worn in a shoulder harness, or fixed on a tripod.

Cine-cameras are very much cheaper than video equipment, but the films can only be used once. There is no way of correcting your mistakes with a cine-film, unless you are prepared to edit them, so you must plan your sequences very carefully.

With both video and cine equipment, sound is likely to be of poor quality if the film is made in a noisy classroom or playground. In the case of cine, it is complicated and expensive to attach a different sound-track to the film. You would do better to make a silent film, and accompany it by an on-the-spot commentary. If you use video, you can dub a commentary on to the tape after filming, or deliver the commentary as you show the tape-recording.

Costs and feasibility

A Sony Rover portable video set (tape deck, camera and monitor television), costs around £1,400 and the 30 minute half-inch tape costs about £6.50.* Costs would be less from a discount shop or *via* the local education authority, which gets a reduction. Video tapes can be used over and over again and need no processing.

* Prices obtained in December, 1980

The prices of cine-cameras vary according to the quality of the equipment, what you want it to do and the accessories you buy. Cameras which take Super 8 silent colour film cartridges start at £50–60. The film lasts for three and a half minutes and costs approximately £4.50 including processing. For £80–90 you can buy a camera which will take the same length cine film with sound as well. You will need a camera case (starting at £13) and a cine projector. Silent projectors cost around £80; sound projectors start at £125. It is possible to make longer Super 8 films which last for 13 minutes but the camera required will be more expensive.

Many teachers' centres run courses on film-making in schools. The ILEA offers a projectionist's certificate and a video users' certificate to those successfully completing their course.

Some teachers' centres have video or cine equipment which they are prepared to loan. In other instances the wardens or technicians at these centres prefer to come and make the film in the school. This has the drawback that it becomes a more complicated operation, dependent on more people's time and convenience, and so unlikely to become a regular part of school life.

The cost of video equipment is so high that it is rarely within the scope of any individual nursery or primary school, but two or three neighbouring schools could club together and share the equipment. Another possibility is that the educational technology department of the local college of education or polytechnic might be able to loan equipment.

Cine-cameras are cheap enough to be bought out of school or PTA funds. One of the staff or parents might have a cine-camera which they would lend, or use themselves, to make a film. Before buying the equipment, or using equipment which the school already has, it will be worth seeking advice from the technician at the local teachers' centre or audio-visual aid centre or, in ILEA, from a media resources officer, to ensure that your equipment is compatible or will be compatible with anything extra you may need to borrow or hire from them.

Organizing parent involvement

Making and showing films: a staff-parent venture

Making films to be used only within the school does not need tremendous skill—the audience will be very tolerant of the minor deficiences of the film if they are absorbed by the subject matter. It does call for a certain amount of experience and confidence, but the equipment we have suggested is easy to operate and doesn't need an expert. However, the contents of the films do need to be carefully planned, so that the sequences which are filmed illustrate the points which it is intended to make. It's much easier to do all this if two or more people are working together. For this reason alone it is worth enlisting the help of a parent—it's quite likely that some parents in each school are knowledgeable about, or at least interested in, filming. A staff-parent film group, which jointly works out what to make films about, and how to make them, is worth considering. The staff could start by holding a meeting for interested parents. If teachers work with parents in this way, they are likely to give all kinds of help—even financial support—and help in the classroom while the film is being made, and in doing so they will also find out about the school for themselves. When the time comes to show the film, help will be needed from someone who knows how to use the equipment, and who can help to check plugs, leads, projector, screen, sources of light, and black-out.

Content of films

In our project we made films of three types; a typical day in a particular class, a specific area of the curriculum, and films about children's lives out of school. In the first kind of film the camera roved around the class showing the range of work and activities that went on and including, if possible, all the children present at the time. One such film in a nursery might include shots of the parents and children arriving in the morning, or choosing books from the lending library together, followed by shots of the children painting, doing puzzles, playing in the home corner or sand pit, outside on the climbing frame with friends, washing before lunch, or joining in with the group story time. Films can be made to show the children taking part in all sorts of activities which, particularly in the infant school, some parents rarely have the chance to see. Examples are:

- the children in assembly, physical education, music, movement and drama, swimming

- having school lunch, playing in the playground

- reading to the teacher in class, working individually or in a group

- going on outings

Such films can be an eye-opener for staff and parents. For example, seeing the noise and confusion of some infant playgrounds or halls at lunch time, and the various ways in which children respond to the situations, is likely to raise questions among parents and staff about possible alternative methods of organization.

In the second kind of film we focused on specific activities related to literacy and to numeracy. Children were shown learning to use pencils and paint, playing games to encourage hand control, matching shapes and pictures, listening to a story, reading, and so on. These films were shown in conjunction with a display of the relevant equipment, and materials for the parents to see and try out.

The third kind of film we made was concerned with children's lives out of school. Such films can provide interesting material for parents and staff to discuss. These films, probably best made by parents, will be particularly helpful in schools serving multiracial areas. Films of events in the local community which are particularly significant to the children, as well as films of simple evening and weekend activities in the lives of the families, will contain plenty of material to stimulate discussion.

If other schools agreed to cooperate, a film could be made for nursery parents about the local infant school or schools, or one for parents of infant children about the junior school. Not only would this help parents to learn more about their children's future schools, it could serve to widen their knowledge of the education system and the place of nursery and infant education in it.

Reactions to the film

The enthusiasm of the parents has already been mentioned—in our project we found that films were one of the most appreciated forms of communication. The children were remarkably unconcerned by the camera and they rarely looked directly into the lens. Some were initially intrigued by the equipment, but they soon lost interest and turned their attention elsewhere. The staff quickly overcame their camera nerves, especially when they had something specific to do with an individual or group. They found it a very useful way of communicating with parents. It was easier to talk about a child to the parent when they had both watched how he got on with other children, or how he set about work.

A possible alternative: colour slides

If video recordings or cine-films are not possible, then colour slides are worth considering for a parents' meeting. If the shots are carefully chosen, they can illustrate the points to be made in exactly the same way as film. Slides do have the advantage that it is easier to discuss each shot at leisure: on the other hand there is no doubt they are less appealing than film. A good basic camera costs around £50, but a much cheaper camera could be used. Thirty-six transparencies will cost around £4, including processing, although schools are able, through bulk purchase, to reduce this cost. A further possibility is the tape-slide synchronized programme, which requires an automatic 35mm slide projector of the Carousel type, a suitable cassette, and reel-to-reel tape recorder, and a synchronizer. A suitable cassette machine and synchronizer costs upwards of £100. A Carousel projector suitable for tape-slide presentations costs around £200, depending on the lens chosen.

Limitations

Films are undoubtedly a great draw: you can use them to attract parents to your meetings. But if you want to develop a two-way discussion, and build more contacts with parents into your day-to-day practice, you will have to do more than show a film. In other chapters we discuss methods for developing discussion.

Evaluation

● After showing a film, ask parents for their opinions about the most interesting features of it, and ask them for suggestions for further films.

Some hints on film technique

For those teachers or parents who intend making a film or video recording we offer the following hints on technique.

1　Never use a video camera to shoot against the light. If you do you will get perfectly exposed exteriors and silhouettes in the classroom.

2　Avoid the use of the zoom unless absolutely necessary.

3 Try to keep your shots static unless it is absolutely essential to move a camera to follow the action.

4 If you must pan (i.e. move the camera to the left or right) do it very slowly and always keep the camera running when you come to the end of the pan for at least two or three seconds. This avoids a kind of sea-sickness effect—the feeling that you are about to fall off your feet!

5 When using a zoom lens always follow the basic rule whether in film or video—zoom in, focus, pull back to the required frame. If you do this the picture will remain in focus at any stage along the zoom. If you do not it is possible to zoom in and zoom completely out of focus.

A classroom visiting time

Most parents are eager to know what goes on in their children's school and anxious to understand the teacher's methods. This is especially true of those parents who have no experience of the British education system. One way to achieve this is to show parents the class in action. Many nursery and infant schools do, in fact, issue an open invitation to parents to drop in whenever they have the time. Usually only a few parents take up this opportunity, either because they are at work or because they do not feel sufficiently at ease in the school. Even if they do come, we found that just watching what goes on, or even joining in the activities, doesn't necessarily mean that parents understand the purpose of them. For example, they do not know whether the activity is being carried out just for enjoyment or whether it also forms part of a planned learning sequence.

The role of play in nursery and infant education, and the modern approach to mathematics, mystify most parents. Vague assurances that children 'learn through play', or that they are acquiring fundamental concepts, do not easily convince them.

Evening meetings when materials are displayed and explained, and parents can try them out themselves, are one approach to the problem. They do not, though, satisfy the parents' desire to see the school in action. So there is much to be said for a regular visiting time, when parents know that they are welcome and expected, and that they can ask questions in the knowledge that the staff have time to talk to them. (Such an arrangement need not, of course, preclude parents visiting at other times if the staff are willing.)

Aims

● To enable parents to watch class activities

● To provide an opportunity for staff to explain the school activities to parents

● To help parent and child communicate about the child's life at school

A weekly visiting hour in a nursery class

In one of our nursery classes parents were invited to come for the last half hour of the morning or afternoon session, once a week. This meant altering the nursery routine since usually the session ended with a group story, and by the time the parents arrived most activities had been cleared away. On Tuesdays the children had their story earlier and continued their other activities until the end of the session so that parents could see them in action.

Parents who came were able to join in the activities, observe their own and other children and talk to the staff and to other parents. The staff tried to be free to talk to them at this time. Parents could join their own children and friends in a game, watch them paint, make a model or read a story. The staff were able to demonstrate on the spot how certain apparatus was used and to answer queries which might be forgotten by the time a more formal opportunity to ask them arose. In this way parents could get more direct knowledge of what the children did, which they could use in discussions with the staff, with other parents, and with their own children. On an average 14 parents came to each session, often bringing babies and toddlers.

There were very few occasions when the parents' presence was disruptive. Very young babies were usually left in their prams in a corner of the nursery or in the corridor outside. The toddlers enjoyed the chance to be with their brothers or sisters and to play with some of the nursery toys. Reorganizing the routine did confuse a few children initially but Tuesday soon came to be called 'the upside down day'.

Other possible ways of organizing visits from parents

In the bustle of nursery activities, where children are free to move around as they wish, and there is usually plenty of room, visiting adults cause little disturbance. In the infant classroom their presence may be more distracting as both staff and space will be in shorter supply. Even in a nursery classroom if the classroom is small the teacher may not want or feel able to cope with a large number of parents at one time. However, there are several ways in which the idea of a 'visiting time' can be adapted to different needs and circumstances.

● A time can be set aside each week when a few parents are personally invited to visit the class. At this time individual or group activities can be planned for the children which leave staff free to give some attention to the visitors. Obviously help in the classroom to deal with some of the children's demands is needed to allow the teacher time for parents. It may be possible to enlist the help of the welfare assistant, or the head, or another parent to keep things running smoothly during this time. This arrangement will enable each parent to visit the class by invitation once a term.

● There can be regular open mornings or afternoons (for example, once a term, or half-term) when parents are invited to come in at any time during the half-day to watch the children at work. This is especially valuable if, at the end of the session, the staff discuss with the parents what they have seen. If the open sessions coincide with the completion of a piece of group or class work, the staff can explain their purpose in carrying out the activity, and recount its development, and parents can hear about their own children's contribution to the final result.

● Parents can also be invited to watch specific activities such as PE, assembly, a baking session or mathematics in action. In the case of reading or mathematics it may be helpful to tie in an evening meeting with a subsequent visiting time. At the preliminary meeting the teacher can show the parents the aids and books she uses, describe their functions and answer questions. Later, the parents can be invited to come to the class and see the children using the apparatus.

● Parents can be invited to stay for a while at the beginning of the session or to come early at the end, for a special event, for instance to see the children acting a play based on a class story, or using masks they have made. There is less opportunity to talk to staff on these occasions but it enables parents to see a part of the class activity that is normally only seen in the formal setting of the end-of-term concert. In all these instances staff could explain to parents why the particular story has been chosen, or why masks have been made and what they hoped the children would gain from the experience.

● During the week of their child's birthday, the parents can be invited to spend part of the day joining in or observing their child's activities, ending with whatever birthday ritual the class enjoys.

Organizing parent involvement

● Groups of parents can be invited to have lunch with their children at school. This is particularly valuable for parents with children in a half-day nursery class, for it allows the children to experience the school lunch-time that many of them will soon be coping with. The parents are able to see at first hand how lunch-time is organized and how they need to prepare their child for it. This arrangement can become a regular part of school life on certain days. For example, once a week a few parents can join their children for lunch with one or two of the staff. Ideally, this will be their child's present teacher and nursery assistant, and, towards the end of the term or year, the person who will be their next teacher.

Parents need to be informed verbally and by letter when the visiting arrangements start and it is helpful to put posters up to remind people the day before visits. Parents may feel ill at ease when they go into a classroom and they need to be welcomed as they arrive, with a brief word about where their child is and what he is doing. Staff need to plan in advance how they will use the visiting time—to circulate among parents, to demonstrate a particular activity, to see particular parents etc.

Visits by minority group parents

For non-English speaking parents, it would be particularly valuable to organize a series of visits to the classroom with an interpreter. At the end of the series, parents' questions can be put to the teacher *via* the interpreter.

A series of planned visits would also be useful in schools where there are parents who, while English speaking, have had no experience of the British educational system. These visits could serve as part of an introductory programme to the school. Parents and staff could meet at the end and discuss what has been seen. If a series of visits were planned in this way, it might be useful to structure them—for example, one could be concerned with mathematical activities, another with the teacher's role in the classroom.

Limitations

Not all parents, especially fathers and working mothers, are free during the day, so evening meetings are also needed. Moreover, the visiting time is not a suitable occasion for detailed, personal discussion about individual children, and is not intended to be a substitute for that. But the more parents and staff know and understand about each other and the school the more fruitful discussions about individual children are likely to be.

Evaluation

● Keep records of who comes. At the end of each term the teacher needs to find out which parents have not visited the school, and ask them if any other day or time would suit them better.
● Ask for comments, perhaps in the suggestion box, from those parents who did come—for instance about any other activities they would like explained or demonstrated.

12

Working with parents

Outings and educational visits

Outings offer a welcome break in the school routine to both teachers and children, and frequently parents are asked to accompany classes on outings. In fact, schools are often dependent on parental help in bringing the adult-child ratio to the level required by the authority. However, parents and outings are not always a successful combination; at the end of the day teachers and parents may feel critical rather than friendly towards each other. This is often because of confusion between the role which parents see themselves as having and that which the teachers would like them to play. Further, parents may misunderstand the teachers' aims, which indeed may not have been clearly communicated to them. They may see the outing primarily as a nice chance to get together with friends and neighbours, or see their role as providing a treat for the children and indulging them with a plentiful supply of sweets and ice creams. The teacher may feel frustrated because the intended 'educational value' of the visit is not achieved; packed lunches, sing-songs, the coach ride, seem to dominate the day.

Yet since this kind of outing is looked forward to by parents, children, and many teachers, it may be best seen as a worthwhile 'fun' event, where the primary aim is for everyone to get to know each other better in a light hearted atmosphere. Outings such as trips to the seaside, picnics in the country, visits to pantomimes, parks and zoos might be better organized by parents, with the help of the school where required. But if the aim of the outing is to provide particular educational experiences relevant to class work or interests, a different and more organized form of parent help is needed. In this case the aims of parent involvement and the role parents take are similar to those discussed later ('Parents working in the classroom' pages 175–87). The number of parents able and willing to take part in this kind of outing may be small, but their help can be invaluable.

Aims

● To provide a shared educational experience for children, teachers and parents

● To enable parents to contribute to the curriculum

● To enable teachers and children to benefit from the parents' knowledge of, and contacts in, the locality

Guidance for parents

If these aims are to be achieved, the parents' role must be much more than simply boosting the adult-child ratio. Parents must be working with teachers and children to achieve specified aims. To take on this role parents need clear guidance—they need to know what the purpose of the visit is, what is to be seen, done, talked about, how the experience relates to classwork, and so on. They will also need guidance on how a group of children are expected to behave out of school. Because of their experiences with their own children, parents are likely to be able to contribute usefully to all these decisions if they are consulted.

Organizing parent involvement

Before the visit

● Ask for suggestions of places to visit

When the venue has been decided,

● Invite parents to discuss with staff all aspects of the outing

● Try to arrange for some parents to make a preliminary visit with a member of staff

● Allocate specific children to specific parents who will accompany them

● Arrange for parents to work with 'their' group of children before and after the visit, for preparatory and follow-up activities

This is particularly helpful since it is the accompanying parents not the teacher who directly shares the experience with the children assigned to them. If this is not possible it is helpful if parents can at least meet 'their' children beforehand. During the project we found that prior discussion of cost, suitable dress and food, and agreement about sweets and ices, as well as discussion about aims, eliminated many of the usual problems.

After the visit

Parents who are unable to attend may like to receive an account of the visit from the person who accompanied their child. We found parents' interest was quickly aroused when a display of photographs with explanatory captions was made after the return to school. We used instant polaroid film. It was helpful to have a parent as 'outing photographer'.

We found that parents welcomed suggestions for following up the children's interest at home, such as loans of books and pictures, list of other places for weekend visits, TV programmes related to the interest, topics for drawing and writing about, things to look out for in the locality. If there is a class newsletter, these items could be included.

Mini-outings

There are many advantages in having outings in the neighbour-hood for small groups—up to four or five children—as a regular part of class activities. How such outings are organized depends on the availability of parents. In one of our project schools the parents who were working in the classroom on a regular basis were able to extend their contribution by taking out small groups of children; in another, a group of parents planned a series of outings for the term. Such a parent group can survey the area to discover places of interest, plan visits with the teacher, and take responsibility for informing other parents and obtaining their help. This group can also produce a list of local places of interest for family visits during weekends or holidays and distribute it to parents. As with the bigger class outings, parents need first to discuss with the teacher what the purpose of the outing is, what the children may get out of it, and the kinds of things to direct their attention to.

There are also a number of parents who, while unable to give frequent help, can contribute occasionally. A particularly valu-able example of occasional help is that of parents taking a small group of children to visit their workplace. Visits of this kind can bring the adult world to children more vividly than is possible if they stay within the school walls.

Outings of this kind require parents to give permission for their children to leave school premises with another parent, and may also require additional insurance.

People and places visited on mini outings

This list gives an indication of the range of outings planned in our project, which derived from knowledge of parents and other local people. In multi-racial areas visits to local minority meeting places, such as temples, synagogues, shops, and homes are particularly important in ensuring that all the children receive a multicultural education.

Although the children went in the local shops regularly with their parents, a visit planned with the cooperation of the shopkeepers proved an entirely different experience for both children and parents; the local supermarket agreed for instance to show the children its loading bay and store room. Two mothers who worked an allotment let the children help reap some of the 'harvest', showed them the garden tools, and so forth. A group of children visited a relative of one of the parents who lived on the top floor of a tower block of flats. Another group visited a pigeon loft owned by one of the parents. Some children were taken to the local garage, where one parent took the children through the car wash in her car, and another showed the children how to fill the car with petrol and oil, and how to check tyre pressures. Children helped a mother who worked in the launderette with the service washing. Other children visited a senior citizens' luncheon club.

Some of the children will have already made these visits with their family. But a leisurely visit, in which the aim is to explain and demonstrate to the children, rather than hurry through with preoccupied parents, can be a much more interesting experience.

Evaluation

● Discuss with parents and others involved in the outing what they felt the children gained from the visits; were there any problems arising from the occasion? Do the parents have suggestions for future outings?

Parents working in the classroom

Should we have parents in the classroom?

To some, 'parent involvement' *means* encouraging parents to help in schools. Other teachers who would like closer home-school links may draw the line at having parents working in the classroom. Their objections can be classified as (1) *managerial*—the difficulty of fitting parental help into the daily timetable; the extra time and effort that would be needed to do so; the problem of coping with 'difficult' parents; (2) *professional*—'teaching is a specialized skill'; parents might behave 'unprofessionally', for instance, gossip about children's problems out of school; (3) *trade union based*—unpaid help shouldn't be used when there are many unemployed teachers; (4) *educational*—parental help is unneccessary, because the teacher can educate the children adequately without it; parents are not sufficiently educated themselves to make a useful contribution; (5) *personal*—some teachers are embarrassed by the presence of another adult in the classroom, or feel that the presence of parents would interfere with their relationship with the children, or with their autonomy in the classroom. Finally, it's often argued that in any case very few parents have the time and energy to work in the school.

For one or other of these reasons many infant schools do without parental help or use parents mainly outside the classroom, for instance to help on outings. Nursery teachers are more likely to invite parents to work with children, but usually only a few parents take up the offer. In the course of our project we found one reason for reluctance on the part of the parents was that those who had worked in the classroom had not always enjoyed the experience or found it worthwhile. Other parents had reacted more positively; we will discuss the possible reasons for this difference later.

In the face of all these problems what is the case for having parents work in the school? We certainly don't consider it as the key form of parent involvement, if only because the proportion of parents likely to be involved in this way is small. Most fathers work during school hours, increasing numbers of mothers are going out to work, others are busy with younger children or simply value their time without children around. Nevertheless, we think that there are two important reasons which make it worth while to try to organize some help from parents. First, having parents work in the school is perhaps the best way for them to understand what is going on, and find a basis for discussing their children's education with the staff and with their own children. If organized in the right way, this will increase parents' knowledge about the school, give them the satisfaction of making a contribution to their children's education in the classroom, and increase their interest and their support for the school and the staff.

Secondly, if parents work in the school, the school is able to benefit from the skills and interest of the parents. This is because parents are not just 'an extra pair of hands'. They are likely to have skills, interests, and contacts in the community which are much wider and more varied than those of the staff, simply because they represent a wider cross-section of society than teachers. However many staff there are, they are unlikely to match the parents in the range of interests which they can offer the children. This is particularly the case in multi-racial schools, where parents are an essential resource for enabling teachers to provide a multi-cultural curriculum.

For both these reasons we see parents not as a cheap alternative to employing more teachers, but an important potential supplement, or resource to the life of the school, which is at present under-utilized. Of course, not all parents can, or will want to, work in the school, and pressure should not be put on reluctant parents to do so. But all classes are likely to have some parents who are both able and willing to make a contribution.

Organizing parental help in such a way that both the parent and the school can be enriched is admittedly not easy. It can only succeed if the teachers are clear about their aims, recognize the potential benefit to the school of the parents' help, and recognize the parents' need to find the experience satisfying.

Aims

The suggestions we make in this chapter are made on the basis of our work in trying to achieve two main aims through having parents work in the class.

● To provide parents with enough experience of the class work to have a basis for discussion with the teacher about their child's progress and the work of the school

● To enable the class to profit from the skills and interests of the parents and to enable the parents to share in their child's school education by contributing in this way

Organizing parental help

Before starting on this venture teachers need to look at how best parents' contributions can be organized within their particular class, taking into account routine, timetabling, space, staffing and so on. They may want to have a rota of parents, or regular days or times when parents come in, or it may suit them better to invite parents to come in when they need any particular help, for instance when they are covering a particular topic which they know a parent could help with. Some teachers may be prepared to use the help of parents whenever the parents are free.

A regular weekly visit from a parent might enable an activity to be carried out which otherwise couldn't be provided, like football, music, or a mini-outing, gardening, dancing, or carpentry. Or, if one or two parents who are happy and able to work with groups of children will always be in the class on a particular afternoon, some teachers would be willing to leave the class in the care of a nursery assistant and these parents in order to do some home visiting. Another possibility is to arrange that parents come at a certain time each day—for example after lunch to hear children read or to read to them, or at lunch time in the nursery to enable more children to stay for lunch. Parents will be reliable if they realize that both the staff and the children really depend on their presence at that time. We found that what many parents liked best was to work regularly with the same child, or the same small group of children, so that they could get to know them and watch them develop. Teachers with non-English speaking children in their class may get regular help from parents in the teaching of English (see page 56). In the classes in our project we found that the number of parents willing to work *regularly*, at least once a week, varied from one to 12 per class, depending mainly on the size of families and whether mothers worked. Fathers on shift work may be able to join a rota, but most fathers are likely to be able to offer only occasional help.

Once the names of parents willing to help regularly have been collected, it is useful to have an initial meeting with them. On this occasion they can get to know each other, discuss what they would like to do, and the teacher can explain the kind of regular help that she would find useful. If this parent group continues to meet from time to time, further suggestions can be collected from them, the teacher can explain in greater detail what is going on in the classroom, and the parents' queries and comments can be discussed.

If the group is large, it may be worth nominating one person as their specific 'link' with the staff between meetings, to coordinate activities and suggestions and pass on any queries or dislikes. We found one mother had been asked by the teacher to take a group of children for cookery each week. The mother didn't want to do this, but didn't like to refuse, the staff thought she enjoyed it and it was several weeks before the misunderstanding was resolved. Other mothers who had been asked to read to children disliked this task, but felt unable to say so.

The majority of parents either haven't the time or don't want to commit themselves to a rota system, but may come for occasional sessions, especially if they realize they can offer something worthwhile. The teacher may be covering a particular 'topic' to which a parent could contribute—people's jobs, babies, pets. For example, parents may come in their nurses' or bus conductors' uniforms, and show the children some of the tools of their trade. Other parents may have something of interest to show and explain to the children—a motorbike, a guitar, budgerigars, houseplants, photos of recent holidays or of their own childhood. Others may bring a loom or a sewing machine, and show the children how to use them. Parents from minority groups can show the children something of their culture, like dancing or cooking, and can organize celebrations of their national and religious festivals. Parents who would not come regularly to school can sometimes be relied on to help on special occasions—for example to help prepare for a party at Christmas. Other parents, whether they come regularly or occasionally, will prefer to work with the usual class activities, hearing reading, reading aloud to small groups, helping children with puzzles. We found most parents preferred to have a set task rather than being asked to 'generally join in'. Not all parents enjoy joining in children's play, and they often feel awkward in a class unless they have something specific to do.

Inviting parental contributions

The better the teacher knows the parents of her class through frequent chats and visits, the more likely she is to find ways in which they can contribute, and the more willing they will be to come into the school. Parents may first be invited to help, and asked if they have any special hobbies or interests which could enrich the curriculum, during the initial home visit. Once parents realize the kind of help which is wanted they are likely to make their own suggestions. The invitation to help can be repeated in the prospectus, and, once the child starts school, verbally, by newsletters and by notices.

In addition, or in preference, to asking parents to share their interests with the children, some of our project teachers made out a list of activities they wanted help with—such as sewing, football, cooking—and asked parents to 'sign up' for an activity which interested them. It's important to make it clear whether regular or occasional help is wanted, or both, and whether or not parents may come to help without prior notice.

Making parents feel welcome

In talking to parents, we found that they sometimes felt lost or unwelcome in the classroom. They were not always greeted on arrival, and staff sometimes disappeared for coffee or lunch without them. If parents aren't allowed in the staff room it is of course an elementary courtesy to provide coffee and lunch for them and to join them on these occasions.

When parents come in, they should be greeted, made to feel welcome, and introduced to other staff and the children. It is important to make sure that they know what to do during the session, where they will do it, and with whom. If certain materials are needed, they need to be shown where to find them. If a parent has her own idea of what to do, the teacher will first have had to work out with her what materials she needs, which children will be with her, and whether they can choose to come or not. The parent will need some idea of what she is to aim at, and what she should expect of the children. For example, if she is to hear reading, should she always correct mistakes? If she is to do cooking, is she to let the children weigh out the ingredients, and how much help should she give? What does the teacher want the children to get out of the experience? If a parent is expected to come regularly, it is worth spending time with them on their first visit, perhaps working with or near them in the classroom.

There are times in the day when all the children are occupied with the staff—like 'register', or story-time. Parents often feel awkward at these times, and if they talk to each other they may distract the children. It helps if they know what to do at these times—at story time they might listen to the story with the children, or tell a separate story to a small group of children, or they might carry on with some activity of their own. Some parents prefer to come in to do a specific prepared task and then leave. It is helpful to make clear whether this is acceptable and whether or not they are free to stay as long as they want.

Space and numbers

If the room is small, and additional adults are hard to accommodate, there may be extra space that can be used, like the hall, playground, a corridor or medical room. If there is more than one member of staff in the class it may be preferable for one of the staff to take a group of children out to an alternative area, rather than asking the parent to do so. Not only may parents be apprehensive of being isolated, but many of the parents in our project enjoyed seeing the children and what went on in the classroom. In one of our project nursery schools there were sometimes seven or eight parents working at one time, but in others this would have been physically impossible to achieve. However, even a small infant classroom can usually accommodate one or two extra adults. The number of adult helpers desirable depends not only on space, but on management considerations. Some teachers find one or at most two parents at a time all they can, or wish to, cope with, others find a use for any extra help they can get. It is best to start with one or two parents and build up numbers as the need arises, space permits, and as volunteers come forward. If the teacher finds she is getting harassed, or spending most of her time organizing help, then she will need to reduce the number of parents or have a more balanced group—some parents need more guidance than others, and some activities need more organizing. With extra adults in the class the teacher will have fewer children to work with. The parents' presence will thus release her to work with individual children, to do activities that need close supervision, or to spend time observing the class—something that many teachers never manage to do.

Are there some jobs which parents shouldn't do?

This depends on how the teacher feels about 'lay' workers in the classroom. Many teachers will allow parents to do cooking but not to hear children read. This judgement is based on the assumption that hearing reading is a 'professional' activity, while cooking is not. Yet hearing a child read material that a (professional) teacher has judged to be appropriate for that child is no more professional than helping the child to cook, when the child must read the recipe, weigh ingredients, learn about cooking processes and work out the cooking times. Both of these are teaching activities, and the cooking activity is in fact considerably more complex. If the teacher is going to have parents working with children at all, then she needs to communicate to the parent the aim of the activity, the steps to be taken, how to deal with errors, and so forth. *Her* special expertise resides in knowing what to do and how to do it; she does not need to carry out all the steps herself.

There are some activities which some parents will be better at than others. Some will prefer working with individual children, others with a group. Few parents would want to take on a whole class, or would be able to do so.

Parents helping in the infant school

Our project took place in nursery classes where children usually chose their activities from a variety planned by the staff. There was no disruption in having parents come in and organize other activities or withdraw a child for a particular activity. We found that the organization of these classes lent itself to having parents work in the classroom, and this would also be true of an informally organized infant class.

There are, however, possible difficulties in involving parents in infant classes, however informally organized, for example the dictates of timetabled activities, such as PE, TV, assembly; the fact that some teachers will object to parents teaching or helping with reading or mathematics; the likelihood that fewer parents will be available, because mothers are likely to go back to work once the children start in infant school.

On the other hand, the infant teacher has some advantages over the nursery teacher. Many infant children will be able to ask for help, find the necessary materials and cooperate more with parents without constant guidance from the teacher. Moreover, infant children are more likely to be able to sustain activities which parents introduce over a longer period. For example, a parent can teach needlework stitches, which children can continue and practice without the parent being there.

Problems that may arise when parents work in the classroom

Difficulties may arise when teachers, children and parents are working together in the class. Some are due to the increased number of adults, some are more to do with particular personalities. Not all teachers will meet the problems we mention, and not all teachers will see them as problems. How they are dealt with depends on the teacher and who is involved. It is difficult to give more than guidelines; some children may take advantage of the increased number of adults by playing one off against the other, e.g. having been told not to go outside by one adult a child may ask another, who gives permission. Children and parents need to know what the class rules are, when permission is necessary, especially where the 'rules' change with the vagaries of the weather, as in the example above.

One difficulty commonly raised is that some parents are not suitable or desirable to have in a classroom because of their personality or behaviour. For example, a parent may be domineering, or may try to do everything for the children, or may use bad language. For this reason, some teachers will not issue an open invitation to parents to help them, but only invite those parents with whom they feel at ease. This is a very understandable point of view, but other teachers who don't want to reject some of their children's parents have found it possible to steer them to the kinds of work where their behaviour will be less of a problem. For example, a more forceful parent may be better at organizing groups for games where the children need to learn and adhere to a set of rules (like ball games, cards, or games like 'follow my leader') rather than working with a particular child who is likely to feel over-whelmed. The problem of a parent doing everything for the children often arises because of the parent's uncertainty about what is expected. It can be avoided if all parents are given clear explanations of the point of the activity and what parent and child are expected to do. Many parents in fact think they have to demonstrate cooking when they're asked to come in and 'do cooking'. We found that parents welcome guidance—what to do if a child doesn't know a word when reading, or whether all children are expected to button their own coats. If parents swear or smoke, it is possible to point out that the school has rules on these matters, and ask them to adhere to them.

Some parents may be unclear about their role in matters of discipline, for instance what to do if a child doesn't do what they ask, or whether they should intervene in a dispute between children. This problem can be solved if parents know how the teacher would deal with the situation. It could be discussed with volunteer parents in meetings as well as individually.

Some parents and teachers think that children will be upset by their parents' presence in class, or that other children may be jealous. We found this happened rarely, and was less likely to happen if the teacher explained to all the children that some parents come to work in school while other parents worked elsewhere. It is also helpful not to make the fact that a parent is coming into class a major event for the children. In the nursery, settling in time will get parents and children used to the idea of parents working in the class. If a problem does arise, it is best to try to discuss it with parent and child, and agree on how to deal with it. Putting the problem off by telling the parent not to come in for a while rarely works. When problems are discussed at meetings of parent volunteers, other parents can help by telling how they avoid difficulties. However, it does take time for many children to get used to their parents coming into class, and if a parent comes in only occasionally it would be unreasonable to expect the child to act as if it were an everyday occurrence. The teacher and parent may have to tolerate some 'showing off' or clinging behaviour. We found that parents need to be warned that this might happen and that the teacher didn't mind. Some parents were embarrased by their child's 'playing up', and without this reassurance they would have been reluctant to come in again.

What does the parent get out of helping in the class?

It is important for teachers to be aware of parents' reactions to the experience. We found that many parents had criticisms or worries about their experience of working in class, but only in one school did they air their problems with the teacher, and this was only when the teacher organized a discussion for the purpose. Many problems are avoidable if careful planning is done beforehand, and if the teacher regularly reviews and evaluates what is happening. This is why holding regular discussions with the parents informally over a cup of coffee about what they've been doing, and how they found it, is very important.

Organizing parent involvement

In our project, we found that what most parents liked best about helping in the class was the feeling that they were making a valuable contribution. Examples of this were: helping when the assistant was ill, or the teacher left the class to make home visits, teaching English to non-English speaking children, showing children how to do unusual arts and crafts which the staff could not teach them, helping with an activity which couldn't have taken place without their help, such as taking children swimming, or coaching in football. What they *disliked* was the feeling that they were not being useful, for instance being asked to sit at tables while children did puzzles, or to keep an eye on children in the playground. Equally, they disliked vague suggestions that they play with the children or 'join in'. They also disliked being uncertain how to carry out an activity—how much help to give children, how much pressure to put on them to persist or, if they were talking to a group of children about one of their interests, how long to talk. They also felt resentful if the staff went off to have coffee in the staffroom without them.

Limitations

In some areas very few parents will be able or willing to work regularly in the class. But if the teacher knows her parents, and can make them feel that they are really welcome, many more will come in occasionally, perhaps when they have a day off work or have a spell on night shift.

Evaluation

● Have a register and ask parents to sign when they leave, with a note of what they did. Explain to them the reason for this. After half a term see if any have stopped coming. There are bound to be some, as younger children change their sleeping habits, or mothers take jobs, but some may stop because they have encountered problems, or felt bored, or dissatisfied. For this reason it's important to have regular informal meetings with the parents who help. Satisfactions and dissatisfactions on both sides can be aired, and suggestions for extending or changing the way they work can be discussed.

A library hour for parents and children

School lending libraries are usually set up for an excellent reason—to provide children with a supply of good quality books to take home. They are particularly needed in areas where the public library has failed to attract children, where there are no local bookshops, and where children don't have many books in their homes. The school may hope not only to provide books for the children, but also to increase parents' interest in children's books, and in their reading progress.

Libraries like this tend to be modelled on the public library system. Books are issued as quickly, conveniently and frequently as possible, but records of what the children borrow are rarely kept. A few parents may act as volunteer librarians, but apart from this, parental involvement is likely to be minimal.

Lending libraries *can* be organized so as to fulfil an extra function—they can not only supply books, but serve as a focus for involving parents in the life of the school. For some teachers who want to start involving parents more fully, a library hour may be the most fruitful way to begin.

The essence of the library hour is that once a week, for the first or last hour of the school day, the class is given over to books and reading activities, with parents participating. Parents are invited not only to choose books with their children, but to stop and browse, read to their children, and talk with other parents and staff. It is an occasion for both parents and teachers to learn more about children's books, and about ways in which they and the children can use and enjoy them.

The library hour also provides an opportunity for individual

Organizing parent involvement

discussion, between parents, and between parents and teachers, in an informal setting. Parents know that teachers are free to talk to them at this time, and teachers know that there will be a number of parents present whom they can consult.

Aims

● To provide parents and children with a supply of books
● To enable parents and teachers to exchange knowledge and experience about using children's books
● To provide a setting for staff-parent discussion
● To provide a setting for parent-parent discussion

These aims will be most effectively achieved if each class has its own library hour. A library for the whole school can't provide the kind of intimate setting in which parents get to know each other and the class teacher. Further, staff can't help children choose books effectively unless they know them well, and it is not easy for staff and parents to have useful discussions about books unless they know each other, as well as the child.

Setting up and running the library hour

It is important that parents and teachers start by discussing the aims of the library hour, and work out together the best day and time to hold it. If many mothers work part time during the day it may be possible to have the library at the end of the day, after school, or before school starts. In schools where many mothers work full time a library hour may not be feasible.

Parents can be involved in selecting books, and can help to decide how to organize the library. Some may have little experience of children's books, others may know more about them than the teacher. All will have an intimate knowledge of their child and his interests, and his life out of school. In this situation, teachers and parents can share and benefit from each other's knowledge and experience.

After informal discussion with parents about the best time to hold the library, it is useful to call a meeting of interested parents to discuss how to set up and run it. At such a meeting some parents could be asked to accompany staff on a visit to the school library service, to a children's library, or to a bookshop, in order to draw up a shopping list of books. Librarians will usually give advice on selection, and most will arrange for schools to borrow books from them for a class library. In some cases, however, it may be necessary to raise funds, or apply to the PTA, or ask the head for part of the school capitation allowance.

Although three books per child is adequate, more than this is desirable, so that children and parents can borrow several books at a time. It is clearly important when choosing books to ensure that a wide variety is available, and that the books are appropriate to the needs and experiences of all the families in the class. In a multi-cultural society, it is important to provide Asian, African and Indian folk tales, as well as the traditional European ones. It's also worth looking for books which depict both black and white families in urban settings, mothers who go out to work, and children who live with single parents, to counterbalance the suburban world reflected in books like *Topsy and Tim*. If some of the parents in the class don't read English, it may be possible to find children's books in their native language. The parents, local community workers, and the children's librarian at the public library may have ideas about where to obtain children's books for minority groups.

If books from the class 'book corner' can also be made available for loan, this will increase the supply of books as well as enable children who have enjoyed a book at school to hear it read to them more often at home.

A straightforward system for the storage and checking out of books is needed. We found that a good arrangement for issuing books was to have a card for each child, kept in a card index box or wall pockets. The parent could write the date and name of the book he was borrowing, and cross it off when the book was returned. In this way staff are left to talk to parents, and a record of what each child has borrowed is available.

Arrangements need to be made to allow books to be changed on other days, if a child is absent or forgets to return a book on library day.

The start of the new library can be announced by letters and posters, as well as by personal contact. An inaugural meeting, where the aims and organization are explained, and the books displayed, is an effective way to begin. A talk by the local children's librarian might be an added attraction.

Possible extensions to the library hour

There are a number of ways in which the library hour could be built on, if parents are interested and facilities are available. In one of our project schools, books on child health and development were collected by parents and staff and added to the library for parents to borrow. In another school special displays were arranged from time to time, for instance of books for under threes, or books for parents, or paperbacks for three to five year olds. A local bookshop arranged these displays, and orders were taken for interested parents. It is also possible to organize occasional discussion about books—for instance, 'Are fairy tales bad for children?', 'Children's comics', 'Can books help children to cope with new events, like going into hospital?'

Selecting books for the library, organizing special displays and book sales, and discussing books each week, are likely to make both staff and parents more knowledgeable about children's books. The local children's librarian should be able to suggest ways of developing this expertise further, for anyone especially interested—for example by recommending appropriate books, and by putting the class in touch with the nearest branch of the Federation of Children's Book Groups. The class teacher can also display new books, together with reviews of them from educational journals.

The library hour and public libraries

In our study we found that the provision of a classroom library did not increase the use of public libraries. But only a small minority of parents used the public library in the first place. Schools could help families to use the public library by publicizing it, and by taking groups of parents and children there, perhaps for special story sessions, during school time. This would, of course, fulfil a different function from the classroom library hour, and is not a substitute for it.

The problem of damage to books

In our project scribbling and tearing pages seemed to happen at home when children were left alone with books, and was most frequent in families where the parents hadn't been able to come to the school and perhaps did not fully understand how to use books with young children. There was very little damage done at home in schools which ran a library hour. It may help to visit (taking a selection of books) some parents at home, to explain that children need to look at library books with an older person and have the story read to them.

In some cases supplying scrap paper may stop children writing on the books; in other cases it may be necessary to supply a special book bag in which books can be kept at home.

Torn books need to be mended immediately, but so long as a book is legible, a certain amount of defacement can be tolerated. A perfectly clean book is probably one that has not been used.

Damage is often caused by younger members of the family. One of our project schools tackled this problem by organizing a collection of especially hardwearing or cheap books for the under threes, and issuing them during the library hour.

Alternative ways of organising a library hour

If the classroom is too small to accommodate parents and children, there may be a larger room in the school which could be used for library sessions, each class using it on one day a week. If this also is not possible, it would be worth considering running an ordinary lending library in the corner of the classroom, supplemented by occasional paperback book sales, book displays, and discussion about specific books or types of books with parents.

Evaluating the library hour

● It is helpful to check which books are borrowed most frequently, and which least. This can indicate which kind of books to order in future. It may also suggest other action—for instance if Ladybird books are the most popular, a discussion could be held about this with parents, and the merits of other types of books can be pointed out.

● It is also helpful to see which parents are using the library. Children whose parents don't use the library may in fact have lots of books and story times at home. If this is not the case, it may be possible to see that these children get extra stories at school.

How a library hour was organized in one project school

The class was housed in a large room, and contained 30 children at each session, with one teacher and two nursery nurses. The school served a mainly white, working class area, from a large between-the-wars council estate. A third of the mothers were working, mostly part time.

As soon as the idea of a library had been agreed with the head teacher a meeting was held with the parents. The teacher explained the aims of the library, described the sort of activities the session might involve and what she hoped the parents and staff would do. Parents were asked for comments and suggestions. They brought up questions of possible damage to books and embarrassment at reading aloud in public. Other parents tried to allay this fear and the teacher explained that since children had to be taught to care for books some damage would be unavoidable while they were learning. Parents suggested the kind of books they would like to include (such as books on sex education, counting and alphabet books) and discussed organization and suitable times.

Some of the parents volunteered to set up a thrift shop to raise money for books. Most of the books were lent by the School Library Service, and some were bought from the school capitation allowance. It was decided to hold the library hour from 8.30 to 9.30 a.m. once a week. This enabled mothers to come in for half an hour on their way to work.

Attendance at this initial meeting was not high—about 33 per cent. However, this group formed a nucleus which served to interest the other parents. At the first library session these parents spent time talking to other parents about the library hour, explaining the routine and encouraging them to stay.

Parents and children were reminded the day before each weekly library session. At the beginning of each session staff arranged all the books on tables and shelves and set out chairs in groups around the room. Often a display of books relating to a current interest was made. In one area of the room some table-top activities were put out for children who lost interest in the books. These were mostly used by the toddlers who came with the parents—most of the nursery children sat with their mothers or fathers for a surprisingly long period, looking at books or listening to stories. Those children whose parents did not bring them, or could not stay, chose a book to take home, and sat with a member of staff or another parent. At the end of the session children and staff put away the books and arranged the usual activities for the rest of the morning.

Each term a selection of new books on loan from the local book shop was displayed at a library session and parents put a slip of paper inside any they would like added to the library. The most popular of these were bought with the proceeds from the thrift shop.

All the parents in the nursery class used the library regularly. Two thirds of the mothers stayed for at least half an hour each wek, and 85 per cent stayed for at least a quarter of an hour. These were not parents who at other times spent long in the school—few parents helped regularly in the nursery. Nor were they parents who were in any sense bookish—only 13 per cent of the children were members of the public library when the project started. A questionnaire at the end of two years indicated that the parents enjoyed the library sessions, valued the supply of good quality books, and appreciated the library hour as a social occasion: the only criticisms made were that there were insufficient books available.

Parents as authors*

Involving parents in their children's school-based education presents particular challenges in multi-racial areas. For schools which want to respond to the needs and reflect the culture of the minority groups they serve, parents form an obvious and readily accessible source of help. Yet for a variety of reasons minority group parents tend to stay away from schools. This was the situation in the multi-racial unit, G, in our research project (see pages 41–2). The countries of origin of the nursery children's parents included Cyprus (both Greek and Turkish areas), England, Guyana, Ireland, Jamaica, Mauritius, Nigeria, Pakistan and Peru. Their linguistic skills were impressive—some spoke

* This project was carried out by Heather Sutton.

four languages, most used English at home as well as their native language. We thought that there should be some way in which their extraordinarily varied cultural backgrounds could be reflected in, and contribute to, the school. Yet although almost all of the parents came to the school to watch video recordings made of the class, they did not participate in discussion or take any active role in the nursery. Because of their very diversity the parents in no sense formed a community, and few even spoke to each other.

For these reasons it seemed to us that any worthwhile contribution from the parents would initially have to be obtained on an individual basis. We knew from interviews with them that they were very concerned about their children's education, and would welcome guidance about how they could help them at home. We were also looking for ways to enrich the curriculum of the nursery with the experiences of the children's families. We thought that both these aims might be fulfilled if the mothers could be persuaded to write and illustrate a short book for their own children, where appropriate in their own language. A research officer visited the mothers at home, put forward the idea, and suggested a layout for the book—a picture on each page, with a sentence underneath it—and discussed possible themes. She tried to direct the mothers' attention away from the usual nursery themes, and to convince them that their own and their child's experiences were valuable material for books. Most books were completed during the visit, which took up to two hours.

One mother chose a neighbour to write about: 'Every day Paul goes to see Ellen . . .' Another wrote about her aunt: 'My Aunty Elsie is clever with her hands . . .' A Jamaican mother wrote about her childhood: 'My father had lots of sweet oranges. We pick young oranges and play games . . .' A Mauritian mother started: 'Once upon a time there was a little girl called Sue who lived in this house in Mauritius . . .' The books were refreshingly unstereotyped—a sad event, for instance, would be recounted without a happy ending. The books varied in length between eight and 20 pages.

At first the mothers were rather shy about drawing, but in the end most of them enjoyed illustrating their books. Few families had suitable pens and paper available, so we took along typing paper, and black felt-tip pens. In some families each family member made a book—for example one mother wrote a book in Turkish about her childhood in Cyrus, and the nursery child's two older brothers wrote in English, one about taking their little brother to the park, the other about a family trip to the zoo.

These books delighted the children, but because we wanted them to be used in the school the research officer 'published' them in the following way. She photocopied the illustrations, then, since the original handwriting and spelling were not always acceptable to the school, printed or typed the text under the illustrations. When the mother had written in a dialect of English the original syntax was retained. If the book was written in a foreign language, an English translation was printed underneath. (Another possibility would have been to produce two copies of the books, one in the mother tongue, and one in English.) Each page was then covered in plastic film. The research officer took a photograph of the child, if possible with his family, photocopied this on to a stiff cardboard front cover, and entitled the book *Sean's Book* by Mrs Brown—for instance. These stiff plastic covered books were then placed in the class library, and a copy was returned to the family for use at home.

If a photocopier had not been available, the mothers could have been asked to write their text and draw their illustrations on separate sheets of paper. The research officer could subsequently have printed the text underneath the illustrations, put the pages into plastic pockets and glued the children's photographs on to the front covers. Apart from the home visits, the activity need then take no more of a teacher's time than making a set of work cards.

Clearly, there are a number of ways in which a teacher can use these books—she can read them to the children, lend them out, she can invite the authors to come and read them to a small group of children, and in the infant schools she can use them as very meaningful reading books for individual children. There is no reason why the books should be seen as a one-off event; if encouraged, the parents would have written more.

The parents in this particular class would probably not have responded to the initial suggestion if it had involved making the books in a group. In other schools, however, it might well be possible to organize a workshop where parents could come and combine a pleasant social occasion with book making.

The books have certainly given a lot of pleasure to the parents, children and teacher concerned. They have created a positive point of contact between parent and teacher, and demonstrated to the parents that the school recognizes and values the children's family experiences. An activity of this kind is likely to enhance both teachers' respect for parents, and parents' own self respect. It should also make subsequent home-school communication easier.

This scheme is worth considering by nursery and infant teachers, whether or not they work in multi-racial areas, who want to create more links between home and school, and who would like to see books in their classroom which reflect the children's out-of-school life.

Involving parents in the teaching of reading

Because we worked in nursery schools and classes, our experience of involving parents in the teaching of reading was limited. But during the same period a project concerned with involving the parents of infant and junior school children in the teaching of reading was being carried out by colleagues in our research unit. The project took place in six inner-city, multi-cultural schools, in Haringey, and resulted in a substantial improvement in reading skills. The findings are described in detail elsewhere (Hewison, 1981); in this section Jenny Hewison discusses how parent involvement was organized at the classroom level.

Organizing parent involvement

Aim

● To involve parents in the teaching of reading, in order to improve their children's reading skills.

In other sections of this book the importance of keeping parents informed about how the school teaches reading has been stressed. Parents want to know what methods and books are used, and open evenings and reading workshops are useful for this purpose. But giving parents this information, although worthwhile and important, is not in itself sufficient if one of the aims of the parent collaboration exercise is to improve children's reading skills. For this purpose, parents should be encouraged to become *actively* involved in their children's efforts to learn: most importantly, they should be encouraged to listen to their children read. The Haringey Project showed that parental help of this kind can lead to quite marked improvements in children's reading performance, if it forms part of a genuinely collaborative effort between parent and teacher.

The question may be asked: surely this is asking parents to teach, and the teaching of reading is a job for professionals? Hearing children read is not the same thing as teaching them. It is the teacher who decides what shall be taught and when, what reading materials to use, how much practice is required before moving on to the next level of difficulty, and so on. What a teacher cannot do is give each child more than a moment of individual attention each day. She cannot in fact give children as much time as they need to practise their newly acquired skills. Parents on the other hand can give their children help with reading on a one-to-one basis: the children benefit, both from the extra time spent practising their skills, and from the extra motivation that comes from knowing their parents are interested and want them to succeed.

If they are to give their children the kind of regular reading practice advocated here, then the obvious and most convenient place to do this is at home. From the school's point of view, this means that appropriate reading material needs to be planned and selected by the teacher and sent home with the child on a regular basis. Many schools already send books home, but usually in an unsystematic way—perhaps only with certain children, or only on special occasions. Under these circumstances, parents do not feel that the part they play is an important one, and recognized to be so by the school: consequently they may give the impression that they 'cannot be bothered' to help their children.

Will parents cooperate?

In inner-city schools, low educational standards are often attributed to a lack of parental interest. It is very unlikely however that this is the correct explanation. We found that parents in such areas are almost always very anxious that their children learn to read—they place high value on reading as a skill, whether or not they themselves choose to read for enjoyment.

Apparent lack of interest in education, such as failure to attend open evenings, should not be taken as evidence that parents do not care whether or not their children acquire basic skills. Given a specific task to do for their child, and given encouragement and assurance and the appropriate materials, in our experience most parents are very happy to cooperate with the school and are pleased to be given an opportunity of helping their children.

Making a start

Faced with the task of telling parents about their school's new parent involvement policy, many teachers would automatically think of calling a parents' meeting. Our experience was that for this purpose group meetings are a very poor second best to individual interviews. These need not be formal, or lengthy, and are no more difficult to organize than a large gathering. Individually-written notes, asking parents to come to school for a chat about reading and what they can contribute, produce a much better response than duplicated forms conveying the same information. In some areas it might be appropriate to give each parent of a new entrant to the infant school a pamphlet or open letter describing the school's policy of involving parents, what that meant in practical terms, how the parents' contribution was valued, and so on. However, even if such a pamphlet were used, individual talks with parents would still be necessary to ensure the fullest possible understanding and cooperation.

Individual talks can be arranged as part of a normal open day or open evening, or at times specially set aside for the purpose, or if necessary squeezed in for one or two parents at the beginning or end of the ordinary school day. Most parents respond to individual requests to come to the school, provided that the time suggested does not clash with work or family commitments. A second note may be needed to bring in a few parents who failed to attend the first time; some missing parents may be caught at the school gate; and one or two families in each class may need a home visit, preceded by an explanatory note.

When describing the school's home reading scheme to parents, a point should first be made of reassuring them that their child is not being singled out in any way—because he is behind with his reading, or because he is black, or for any other reason. It should be stressed that parent involvement is a school policy which applies to all children. It should also be made clear that fathers as well as mothers are welcomed as helpers.

If at all possible, parents should continue to be seen individually at least once a term. Some parents will need more support than others, and these can be seen more often, even if only to exchange a word or two at the school gate. We found that these exchanges can achieve a great deal when there is something very specific to discuss. They can also be used to give feedback, and to thank parents for their efforts.

What kind of information and advice do parents need?

Basic information about the books used to teach reading in the school should be given as a matter of course. Efforts should be made to avoid jargon and technical terms like 'scheme reader' or 'phonic method'. Parents can become very confused by the numbering system on reading scheme books, particularly if more than one scheme is used and book 6 from one scheme is brought home this week and book 2 from the other scheme next week. Some parents will appreciate more detailed information than others—a teacher must use her judgement.

As for specific advice on how to hear children read, we found that most parents really do not need very much, and what they do need is more likely to be tips about what to do when their child makes a mistake, rather than advice about the importance of creating the right kind of atmosphere. Contrary to a commonly expressed fear among teachers, very few parents will intentionally push their children too hard; they want the best for their children, and they want them to learn as well as they can.

The few parents who do put too much pressure on their children are more likely to be doing so from lack of knowledge, for example about how long children can concentrate, than from ambition. Reassurance that their children are making good progress, and advice about the duration of reading sessions may be all that is required. If a teacher *is* worried that a child is being pushed too hard, the best thing to do is observe the child carefully in school: if he likes reading and is eager to read in class, and if in general he seems happy and well-adjusted to school, then there is nothing to worry about. If a child shows any signs of stress, then action should of course be taken—not to reject the parent as a helper, but to try and re-direct his or her concern into more productive channels.

The kind of advice that parents welcome most is what to do when their child makes a mistake, or stops reading at a word he does not know. It can be suggested first of all that they wait a moment or two before saying anything, to allow the child time to self-correct, or to work out what the new word might be for himself. It can then be suggested—with examples and even demonstrations if necessary—that the parents prompt their children either to make use of the context to work out what a word might be, or to prompt with the word's initial sound. Prompting by giving letter names should of course be discouraged, and an alternative method suggested instead. Parents may need to be reassured that the teacher does not mind if a child can read words which he cannot spell. Only if things do not seem to be going well is advice necessary about the actual setting up of home reading sessions—about timing them not to clash with favourite TV programmes, about occupying younger children and avoiding interruptions, about praising the child for coming to read when called, about trying to make the sessions a special time when parents and child can share an activity together. Very occasionally, advice might be needed about where to sit—beside the child rather than opposite him— or to avoid catching his eye while he is reading, because it can encourage him always to look for help rather than trying to work things out for himself.

Once a scheme is working well, rules about the timing of sessions can be relaxed a little: as long as parent and child are both enjoying themselves, they can be told to read to the end of a story, rather than stopping at the end of ten minutes. One would not, after all, want to teach children that reading is something you do every other night for ten minutes. Advice of a more general kind about libraries, bookshops, even suggested book titles, can be very welcome to parents of children eager to do more reading at home, either on their own, or with their parents' help.

Classroom organization

As far as classroom organization is concerned, running an active parent involvement scheme does not need to take up a lot of time. The key to success is structure and an established routine. If for example, it is decided that children should take a reading book home every other night, then the class could be divided into two halves, taking books on alternating nights and bringing them back the following day. A mixture of good and weak readers in each half would distribute the work load efficiently.

In addition to the class teacher's normal reading records— what book a child was on, when she last heard him read and so on—it would be necessary to keep a record of what book each child took home, with the dates on which it was borrowed and returned.

A reading card inside the book can be useful, to specify the amount of reading to be done on a particular night. It is helpful if parents get into a habit of ticking a box on the reading card when the evening's work has been done; but too much reliance should not be placed on this kind of information, because many parents who would never forget to listen to reading often do forget to tick a box on a card, particularly if no pen is to hand at the time.

The extra time required to set up a properly organized home reading scheme—working out the best way to keep records, deciding which children should go into which group—soon pays dividends in terms of the children's improved reading progress. Similarly, the extra time spent every day checking books in and out is soon made up when fewer children need to be given special reading help.

The choice of books to send home entirely depends on what fits in best with the school's customary method of teaching reading. Some schools would prefer to send home scheme reading books, or supplementy books, or specially selected library books, or a planned mixture of all three. It is of course important that if a mixture of books from different schemes and other sources is used, then the books should be banded together according to their level. (This applies equally to books used in the classroom. Organization of a school's stock of books is certainly necessary for the efficient running of a home reading scheme, but it should of course have been done anyway.)

The amount of checking of home reading that the teacher does depends on the child, on the parent, and on the level of reading the child has reached. The greatest danger is for teachers to over-regulate, and try to check every word the child reads at home, or only to allow him to read at home material which has already been read at school.

Checking must be a compromise. It is important to make sure that children are not getting into bad habits, or reading without comprehension. Furthermore, *some* checking has a motivating effect on children—they know that the teacher is aware the work has been done, and done well. On the other hand, it is wasteful of teacher time and an unnecessary brake on a child's progress if his teacher insists on hearing every word read again.

The best approach is for the teacher to get to know her children, and their parents, and to tailor her checking to their needs. Some children, probably the weaker readers, will need a full check of all they had read at home. Others will only need a few pages checked; while the best readers will get most benefit from only reading maybe the last page of a story, then being asked to read certain new words, asked what they mean, or asked questions about the story.

Keeping children in small reading groups can aid checking—if all children in a group are given the same reading to do on the same evenings, checking can be accomplished by 'reading round' the group, with additional probes being made as necessary.

Lost books

Once again, structure and routine are vitally important. The aim is to get the children into the habit of taking a book home one night, bringing it back the next day, and repeating this procedure in a regular fashion, week after week. We found that once this routine was established very few books got lost, and fewer still damaged.

Provision of reading materials

Children who practise their reading at home get through more reading material than they would otherwise manage to. As long as they are working their way through a graded series, their need for books can be met by adding supplementary readers, or books from other schemes, to the basic series (see above). Careful planning is necessary however to sustain progress, and enthusiasm, once the graded series has been completed. Moving through the books of a reading scheme is very motivating to children, and also for their parents, because of the visible evidence of progress it provides. At the end of the scheme, detailed structuring all too often gives way quite suddenly to no structure at all. Children may then be expected to choose, read and return library books, with the minimum of guidance and adult involvement: the motivation that came from working to get on to the next book is now gone.

Some parents will provide the informed support necessary to keep their children reading, for instance helping them choose books in public libraries, buying Puffins or Picture Lions. In other cases some of this responsibility must be taken by the school. Children who have finished a reading scheme should still be given set reading to do at home, and the familiar motivating techniques should be employed—giving a group of children the same reading to do each night, grading the books used (including ordinary library books) in some conspicuous way, and so on. Parental help can now be enlisted, not so much to listen to reading as such, but to supervise and make sure that the work is done. The possibility could also be explored of involving parents in reading comprehension exercises given to the child to do at home, and similar activities. Some parents will obviously have more to offer in this direction than others, but all should be encouraged to do as much as they can.

Organizing parent involvement

What about the children whose parents cannot, or will not, help?

We found that almost all the parents with whom we worked not only agreed to help their children, but continued to do so over a two year period. It should not be assumed that mothers of large families, or single parents, or mothers who go out to work, will be unable or unwilling to find time for home reading. Work sent home from school can give parents in these circumstances the opportunity of spending time alone with a child—time which otherwise some might feel unable to justify.

In some schools there will be parents who do not speak English. In other areas, adult literacy among native English speakers is a problem. Once again, it should not be assumed that these parents cannot help their children. A high level of reading skill is not required to help a six year old. We found that parents who cannot read at this level but who can speak English will listen to their children read aloud and correct them if the reading does not make sense. A concerned parent who does not speak English can act as general supervisor while another family member, perhaps an older brother or sister, provides the actual reading help. Quite simply, children benefit if their parents are asked, or assisted to give as much help as they can.

A few parents will probably be encountered who do not, or cannot, help their children as requested, either because of illness, family discord, pressing social problems, or very occasionally just because they choose not to do so. There are far fewer of these parents than many teachers believe, but as long as they exist, their children need to be catered for—perhaps by organizing extra reading tuition in school in the usual way, or by arranging for the class teacher, or maybe even a senior pupil, to spend time giving reading help to each child on a one-to-one basis.

13

Individual consultations with parents

There are all kinds of reasons why parents may become involved in their children's schools—for instance they may want to meet other parents, get to know the staff, take part in the children's schooling, learn about modern teaching methods, or watch their children in another setting. But the prime motivation for most parents is their intense concern to help their own child. This is shared even by those parents who simply haven't the time, energy or interest to go to open evenings, help in the school, or read pamphlets.

For this reason, individual consultations with parents provide, in our opinion, the single most important opportunity for parent involvement. If a school can manage nothing else, it should at least attempt to hold regular worthwhile discussions about every child with his parents. Almost all parents want to find out about their children's progress, and how best to help them, and almost all have opinions about the school, formed on the basis of their children's experience of it. This concern for their own children can provide a focus for discussion about teaching methods, and school organization, and for an exchange of information between parents and teachers, including parents who would be unlikely to be involved in any other way. Further, it is generally agreed that parents have a right to information about what the school is doing for their child, what he has accomplished and what his difficulties are, and that schools have an obligation to give them this information.

The limitations of open evenings and informal chats

Most teachers would probably recognize these obligations, but would argue that in fact opportunities are provided, and that we have overestimated parental concern: 'the parents we most need to see never come to the school' is a perennial complaint. But what kind of opportunities for individual consultations *do* schools provide, and why do many parents not take them up?

In nursery schools, planned consultations by appointment are rare—teachers tend to rely on informal chats with parents as they bring or collect their children. Parents have told us that these chats are rarely informative; comments tend either to be banal ('she did a lovely painting today') or refer to the child in a way which can be confusing or discouraging. For example, the parent may be told 'she's very quiet' or 'she's not very sociable' or 'she doesn't seem very imaginative' when at home the child chatters freely, or plays happily each day with the neighbour's children, or is forever playing 'dressing up' games. We have rarely heard of a teacher who prefaced such comments by asking the parent about the child's behaviour at home, and then went on to discuss any discrepancies between his behaviour at home and at school. Nor do teachers often see these occasions as an opportunity to further their understanding of a child, by asking about his interests and activities during the weekends and holidays.

Infant schools are more likely to arrange open evenings with displays of work, and individual appointments for parents. But these interviews are often disappointing. The setting is usually public, with other parents waiting their turn, and there is neither the time nor the privacy for adequate discussion of the parents' anxieties, or for a full exchange of information. Parents must often make do with a brief report, couched in vague terms—their child is doing 'well' or is 'slow', 'average', 'untidy' or a 'chatterbox'. Although the child's work is on view, the parent has little idea how to evaluate it, and exactly what the child has learnt or achieved during the year is rarely explained. It is hard to say whether the experience of such interviews produces the attitude common among many parents that the education of their children is a matter to be left to the school, but it certainly does little to change it.

Of course, parents can ask for an appointment for a longer private discussion with the head or class teacher. But this arrangement leaves the initiative to the parents, who are fully aware that they are asking for something that is not usual practice, and may fear that they will therefore be considered a nuisance. The occasions when it is the teacher who summons the parents for private discussion are only too often when a child is in trouble—a summons known with dread as 'having to go up to the school'. The explanation for the reluctance of many parents to accept invitations to school is, therefore, in our opinion, that they have not found the experience rewarding, or may indeed have found it decidedly discouraging.

Aims of individual consultations

- To inform parents about what the school is providing for their children, their achievements and progress

- To enable parents and teachers to pool information, ideas and experience

- To enable parents and teachers to plan work and activities for the children

- To enable teachers to explain their aims and methods with specific reference to individual children

Organizing parent involvement

What should be covered in a parent-teacher consultation?

The discussion should be organized round specific topics, rather than generalities, covering all aspects of the child's development. Parents should be given concrete information about how the child has developed over the term, his behaviour and achievements, and the plans the teacher has for the following term. The discussion should include those aspects of the child's learning and behaviour which need particular attention, and the ways both parents and teachers can help.

If positive parent-teacher relationships are to be developed, it is important that parents are regularly given some 'good news' about their child. Comments such as 'I noticed him helping a younger child on Thursday, tying her shoe laces for her,' are gratefully received and remembered. If the teacher is unable to find anything positive to say about the child, then at least she should be able to put forward positive suggestions for a joint plan with the parent to help the child.

If parents are to increase their understanding of their child at school, comments need to be concrete. For example, 'he's not very sociable' is better expressed as 'when a group of children are playing together, he's not sure how to approach them and ask to join in the game'. Discussion could then be about whether he has this difficulty outside school, and how to help him. Or, 'he knows most of his sounds now' would be meaningful if parents could see a list of the 'sounds' referred to, indicating which are known and not known, how they are learnt, why they're important, how they relate to the teaching of reading, the next objective, and games which the parents might play with the child at home to help him learn 'his sounds'.

The individual consultation also provides an opportunity for teachers to discuss their aims and methods in relation to the child in question. Parents should be able to raise their doubts about the value of sand play, ITA or modern maths for 'their Karen' and the teacher should be able to defend herself by pointing to the benefit to Karen of these activities. If the parent feels that Karen should have practice in mental arithmetic, rather than working on 'sets', the teacher should be able to explain what Karen has gained from modern methods. Or indeed, the teacher may consider it appropriate to respond to the parents' anxieties. She might alter her own practice, for instance by adding some mental arithmetic to her curriculum, or she might suggest ways in which the parents could help their child with mental arithmetic at home.

Not all teachers have the confidence, or perhaps the knowledge, to hold these kinds of discussions with parents. They may need help, support and encouragement—from initial and in-service training, from their head, or from their colleagues in the school.

The parents' contribution to the consultation

It is as essential for parents to have opportunities to contribute their knowledge of their children as it is for schools to provide parents with full information about the children at school. Parents are with their children for longer periods of time than the teachers, in a wider variety of situations.

They know how their children fit into family and community life, and they spend time helping them to do this. But the teacher will rarely even see a child from her class outside the narrow context of the school. The parents' knowledge may help the teacher in her work—for example, she may learn of interests which can be developed at school, or she may see an apparently apathetic child in a new light when she discovers that at home he is a very capable cook, or an excellent whist player.

A parent may also be able to suggest explanations for troublesome aspects of her child's behaviour at school, because, for example, she may know that he is terrified of a certain child, upset by being called a 'wog', or bored by work which is not demanding enough for him.

We found that many parents were, unbeknown to the school,

teaching their children 'school' skills; about half of the parents of three and four year olds in all our project schools were trying to teach their children to read or write, or both. Parents of primary children often teach them spelling or multiplication tables, if they feel these skills are not being adequately taught at school. The teacher certainly needs to know about these activities. If the parent feels a need to supplement the teaching at school the teacher must consider this dissatisfaction seriously, and see it as an important and potentially fruitful point of contact. Any teaching the parents do should at least not be at variance with the school's practice. We found, for example, that parents often started by teaching capital letters. In one project school a 'writing workshop' was set up, and parents were shown how to teach the kind of lower case letters preferred by the school.

Until the pattern of exchanging information is established the teacher will often have to ask for information, especially from parents who do not see their children's home activities as relating to those of the school, or whose interest in school is restricted to the children's acquisition of basic skills. However, this situation is less likely to arise if the teachers' aims have been clearly stated, and parents are involved in some discussion of them.

In this context the discussion may cover topics as diverse as eating problems, shyness with strangers, physical skills, relations with brothers and sisters, as well as the usual academic topics.

Materials needed for individual consultations

1 Records in the nursery. In order for the discussion to take the form suggested here, and for topics to be covered in detail, the teacher will need clearly spelt out aims and objectives for each child, with a record of the progress made in achieving them. Although nursery teachers keep records of individual children, these tend either to be couched in vague terms ('hand-eye coordination is fair') or to be detailed accounts of a particular play activity, such as a brick construction or an imaginative game. How many nursery teachers can accurately describe the progress made during the course of a term by each of their children across a number of areas?

For example, what specific advances in motor skills did Mary make in the summer term? How is she developing socially—is she now more willing to take turns, and does she more often join in a game which involves the children in a division of roles? What about her language—is she more often heard to offer explanations, or act out a role in a fantasy game? Has her taste in books or music changed? Are her paintings more mature, and if so, in what way?

In a nursery organized round children's spontaneous play the difficulty for the teacher in answering these questions is very apparent. If the teacher has two part time classes, and is thus in charge of 50 or 60 children, the difficulties may be considered insuperable. Apart from anything else, the child herself may rarely or never choose activities which will demonstrate whether or not she has advanced in certain areas—she may avoid climbing and balancing apparatus, or scissors, or pencils and crayons. In this situation, how is the teacher to monitor the child's all-round development, be aware of the next step she has to make in a variety of areas, consider whether she needs extra help to make it, and decide how to set about the task?

The obvious solution to this problem is the use of some form of standardized test or detailed checklist (such as the National Children's Bureau Development Guide) which can be used at regular intervals with each child. Many teachers of young children are suspicious of these tests, partly because of the not unreasonable objection that many of the items appear trivial, and unrelated to their own aims, and also because they do not cover such important areas as the level of complexity of the child's imaginative play, or the development of reasoning skills. Joan Tough's methods (1976) for assessing children's use of language have been found more acceptable, but relate to only one aspect of development.

Organizing parent involvement

A further difficulty with attempting to assess the development of children in a number of different areas is the time that it takes, particularly for a teacher with two part time classes. In one of our project schools the assistance of the child's parents was sought in making standardized assessments. The parent, after all, has a much wider and more intensive knowledge of her own child than the teacher, and is more likely to know whether, for example, he can hop on one foot or can answer 'why' questions. Involving the parent in the assessment of his child's development has the added bonus of giving the parent a greater understanding of child development, and an interest in observing his child carefully. The assessment need not, of course, take the form of considering whether the child is 'average' for his age, but rather of where he has got to in various developmental areas, and what to look out for next.

In another nursery class in our project, an attempt was made to monitor the children's play in a different way, without using tests. The staff drew up a list of the steps that they expected the children to go through in their use of each of the common play materials, and this list was pinned next to the material, together with the names of all the children. For example, items in the 'large brick area' included:

Makes simple tower/runway
Makes differentiated or patterned structure, with selective
    placement of bricks, e.g. a house or pattern
Makes a series of linked structures, e.g. a farmhouse with walls
Cooperates with other children in making a structure
Knows the names of the various brick shapes

A tick would be put against a child's name when a member of the staff observed her using the material in a particular way.

This method has the advantage of focusing the attention of all the staff, not just the most exprienced, on the stages in each child's development, and what he needs help with next. The material can also be used as a basis for a discussion of the child's development with his parents. But unless the child chooses to use this equipment, records about him cannot be kept. Moreover, skills or advances not related to specific materials but, for example, displayed in conversation, will be missed.

Given present staffing ratios, and a nursery geared to child-initiated play, it is probably impossible for the teacher to keep adequate records of all her childrens' development across a number of areas. In these circumstances she might decide to choose one area of development for each child, such as relationships with other children, or motor development. Teacher and parent could then contribute their knowledge to this discussion.

2 Records in the infant school. The infant teacher's great disadvantage compared with the nursery teacher is that she is single-handed. In a nursery, assistants and students can be of great help in record keeping. On the other hand it is much easier for the infant teacher to keep a constant eye on at least some areas of a child's development, because she is likely to be using a much more structured approach than the nursery teacher. Checklists and progress charts for reading and maths schemes are readily available, or the teacher can make her own. For example, a particular aspect of mathematics can be broken down into a number of steps—as the child masters each step, the item can be ticked off; similarly records of progress can be produced for other areas of the curriculum—reading, music, PE. If the children have set assignments, records of their completion will serve to monitor these aspects of their work. The teacher will still need to keep records of the children's general behaviour and spontaneous play as a basis for discussion with parents.

Keeping examples of the children's work

Showing parents specific examples of the children's work as well as discussing records will aid their understanding, and help the teacher to avoid using jargon and specialized language in the discussion. In the nursery this is most easily done in relation to the children's art work. If samples of each child's paintings or drawings are kept in a folder, they will form a useful basis for detailed discussion with his parents. Again, some teachers will need support and encouragement from more experienced colleagues before entering such discussions.

In the infant school there is usually no shortage of children's writings and workbooks to discuss, as well as art work. However, the common practice of setting them out in the classroom for the parents to examine on their own is not helpful. Parents have no means of knowing what task was set or attempted, what has been achieved, what the aims were, or how much effort or concentration were involved. In discussion, however, the teacher can use the work to demonstrate in a concrete way what the child has achieved, and what his special successes and difficulties have been. Prior to discussion with parents it is useful to confer with all the staff involved with the child, and to look back over the records made earlier. A note of the points raised can be added to the record: it may prove useful in future discussions.

Access to records

Parents are entitled to have access to records kept on their children, and in this context there should be no problem. The records are a basis for discussion, parents will know what is in them and will have contributed to them. They will be to a great extent 'joint' records.

'Home-school notebooks'

Some of our project teachers found it useful to send news about their child to parents who could not get to the school. In one school 'home-school notebooks' were used for a few parents. In this the teacher would mention events and activities that the child had enjoyed or done well at, or new skills he was learning or had acquired. The books were sent home regularly, at least twice a month, and parents added their own comments and news before returning the book to school. The notebook would often be accompanied by particular examples of the work the child had done. It seemed important that the parent and teacher first met to discuss the idea and agree that it would be helpful and welcome. The child was also fully involved, and was usually with the teacher when any comments were written. Some children took pleasure in thinking up things the teacher could write about them. One teacher found time to send a notebook of this kind to a mother in hospital, to keep her in touch with what her child was doing at school.

Finding time and organizing consultations

How is the class teacher to find time for consultations with parents? Ideally, extra staff should be employed by each school to enable class teachers to spend time each week seeing parents at home and at school. Since these staffing levels have yet to be provided, the class teacher will have to call on the head teacher, other teachers without a class, student teachers, nursery as-sistants, other ancillary staff, and the parents themselves, to enable her to hold consultations or make home visits during school hours, or to have free time during the day if evening consultations are made. It may be possible to fit in a half hour consultation during a lunchbreak, or before the school day begins. It may also be worthwhile for the class teacher to reassess her own use of her time. For example, time spent mounting paintings or decorating the corridor might be better used for a consultation, while other parents, assistants or the children themselves mounted the displays.

One nursery class in the project held an intensive two weeks of consultations in the middle of the term. Appointments were made during the day-time where possible—the teacher saw two parents at the beginning and end of each session throughout the fortnight. Consultations were also held on two evenings with those parents who could not attend during the day. There are disadvantages in holding consultations *en bloc*—if appraisals are made throughout the term some aspects of the children's records may be out of date. In addition, daytime consultations will frequently exclude fathers. However, the advantage for the teacher is that she is able to concentrate for a limited period of time on consulting parents, and reorganize her work and commitments for that period only.

In another nursery the teacher invited up to ten parents at a time to give a date and time during the following fortnight when they would be free to discuss their child. When the consultation was fixed, the staff concerned discussed the child together, and records were updated. Afterwards the teacher might then hold a second discussion with staff and add to the record. This method has the advantage that the consultations can be held as soon as possible after the appraisals of the child have been made, with up-to-date records. Parents' views and information can contribute to the current record, and they can participate in the plans being made for the child.

If the nursery assistant has been closely involved in observations and record-keeping she may also be able to share the work of consulting parents. In one school in our project the home visiting and discussions with parents were shared equally between the teacher and the nursery assistant. Most of the children in the class were part time and it was only possible for these activities to take place if the duties were shared.

Language problems

There are particular problems in holding regular consultations in schools where the teachers and some parents have no common language. Many teachers feel the communication difficulties are overwhelming, and that consultations are just not possible. But it is of the utmost importance that these parents have every opportunity for individual and detailed discussion with the class teacher. Parents from minority groups often suffer from special disadvantages, such as a lack of knowledge and experience of British schools. Anxieties and conflicts frequently arise from misunderstandings due to cultural differences. Shift work, long hours, and family commitments may prevent a high proportion from attending school meetings. In these cases, private and personal consultations at home are the ideal means for helping parents to develop positive relations with the school and the teacher, and to give and receive full information about their children and their school lives.

How consultations are organized will depend very much on the availability of interpreters as well as the particular circumstances of parents and staff. Often there is one member of the family with a reasonable command of English who can on occasion be available to interpret. Since home visiting in the evenings will be necessary it is worth considering whether staff hours can be rearranged so that the class teachers can work one or two evenings a week in exchange for one or two free mornings or afternoons. This arrangement requires, of course, additional staff to relieve in the classroom. Special community teachers are employed in some schools for home visits, but they are not in a position to be so effective, as they are not familiar enough with every child's work. It would be more helpful to use extra staff to free the class teacher. This is, of course, primarily a matter for consideration by the LEA or the head rather than the class teacher.

It is worth noting that many parents will make special efforts to come to schools if they are sure that the effort is worth while. In one school in the project with a high proportion of working mothers the majority were able to make arrangements to visit the school when they were given a choice of times, and the remainder were visited at home by the staff.

Organizing parent involvement

Evaluation

● Records should be kept of which parents have been consulted and an attempt made to discover why some parents have not accepted the invitation. Sometimes parents who never answer a letter will be delighted to see the teacher if she calls for a friendly purpose.

● Before the next consultation, it is useful to check on points made in an earlier discussion. Did the parents and teacher carry out the decisions made and were they of help to the child? Had the teacher profited from and used the information given her by the parent? As with all activities, useful feedback can be had from a suggestion box, or from a notice asking for parents' comments, with some specific questions—such as 'Do you find these consultations useful? Could they be improved in any way? Do the times/days suit you?'

14

Involving parents from minority groups

Many teachers find it very difficult to involve parents from minority groups in their children's school education and in the general life of the school. Yet such involvement is essential if schools are to educate all children for a multi-cultural society, profit from the diversity of cultures among the children and parents, and provide equal opportunity for all children.

It will be apparent that much of what we say in this chapter applies to all parents, and all schools. However, there are specific factors which tend to prevent teachers and parents from minority groups developing closer relationships. And in many schools, where the 'minority group' in fact constitutes the majority, the need for parent involvement is particularly pressing.

Some teachers, seeing the poor response of minority group parents to overtures from the school, conclude that the parents are not interested in their children's education. Others argue sympathetically that the parents are so burdened by social problems, poverty, poor housing, long hours of work, and so forth, that it is unreasonable to expect them to become involved.

There is, however, much evidence which suggests that the opposite is the case. For many parents the wish to obtain a good education for their children was a major factor in their decision to emigrate. In general, truancy rates are lower, and the proportion of children staying on at school after 16 higher, among minority group children, and their parents tend to have high aspirations for them. The establishment of supplementary or 'Saturday' schools within minority communities, which provide not only mother tongue teaching, religious knowledge, cultural and traditional activities, but also in many cases supplementary teaching in literacy and numeracy, suggests dissatisfaction with state schooling, and real concern for and interest in their children's education.

Problems of teachers and parents in multi-cultural schools

If the interest is there, why is it difficult for teachers to involve and work with minority group parents? There is no simple answer to this question, not least because of the diversity among minority groups. With some parents, for instance the Spanish and Italian, the main difficulty may be the lack of a shared language; with others, for instance Pakistanis and Chinese, there may be not only language obstacles, but others arising from communicating with people whose cultures are very different and distinct. Communication with West Indian parents is not usually hindered by language differences, nor by the existence of an obviously distinct culture. Instead, a major barrier, present also with Asian groups, may be fear and suspicion, bred by racist experiences in our society. With all these groups there are also likely to be cultural differences in the widest sense—in child rearing practices, and in attitudes to education and schools—which contribute to the difficulty of understanding and communicating.

The most easily identified of these obstacles, which we will return to later, is the 'language barrier'—it is hard for teacher and parent to communicate without a common language. But more subtle difficulties arise from cultural differences which affect parent-school relationships. Minority group parents' expectations of the school are frequently at variance with school practice. Parents tend to expect a formal relationship between teacher and child, when the teacher offers an informal one.

They expect that their children will be made to sit still, and address the staff politely, and that serious punishment will follow lapses in discipline. They are also accustomed to regard schooling as a matter to be left to the teacher, and puzzled by requests to work in the school. On the other hand, in their country of origin the teacher was likely to be no stranger to them, but someone who lived within their community, and with whom they were in daily contact outside the school. The British situation, in which parents are expected to visit and even spend time in the school, but the teacher tends to hurry away from the neighbourhood as soon as school finishes, is unfamiliar to many minority groups.

Despite their inclination to leave schooling to teachers, minority parents are usually puzzled and often antagonized by the 'learning through play' methods of British nursery and infant classes. For example, when we asked the parents in our project if they knew why certain play materials were provided in nursery schools, we found that the majority of Asian and West Indian parents had either no idea, or had developed their own explanations much at variance with the teachers'—for example: 'Water is provided so that children will lose their fear of water,' 'Sand is provided to remind the children about the seaside, which English people are so fond of.' In some minority groups a high value is placed on children looking clean and tidy, and parents' hearts do not warm at the sight of their children wet from water play or covered with paint. West Indian parents often particularly object to the provision of sand, because of the difficulty of brushing it out of tightly curled or plaited hair.

Asian parents are often disappointed and bemused by the apparent absence of systematic English language teaching in most nursery schools. In our project, many Asian parents said that they had sent their children to school to learn English. Not unreasonably they did not all accept the teachers' argument that their children would learn English in the course of normal nursery activities, particularly when the majority of children in the class were non-English speaking.

Not only the teaching methods, but the teaching aims are incomprehensible to many parents. They expect their children to progress as rapidly as possible with reading and writing, at a time when the teachers are intent on developing creativity, imagination, and the provision of varied perceptual language and motor experiences. Attempts by teachers to explain their aims and methods tend to leave these parents unconvinced. Everything in their own experience and culture leads them to believe that their child's future success depends on his acquiring habits of hard work, and on diligent attention to formal skills.

Other difficulties may be caused by schools having inadequate, incomplete or incorrect basic information about children, their families and their lives. Names are sometimes mis-spelt or changed, teachers may not know, or may be misinformed about what language the parents speak, what language is spoken at home to the child, where the parents come from, or what religious beliefs they hold. Additional information about the cultural backgrounds of the children may not be collected or assembled in a very useful way by the school—for instance books about minority cultures are often not available for teachers in the staffroom, and the dates, names, and meanings of religious festivals are not always known. While complaining that minority group parents do not come to the school, very few teachers visit them at home, spend time in the neighbourhood, for instance in the local shops and cafes, or visit the temples, churches, or social centres which play an important part in the lives of the families.

If to this is added the mono-cultural, ethnocentric character of most British schools, the disregard for and tendency to devalue other cultures (in respect of choice of books, pictures, stories, songs, toys, interior decoration, food, clothing and festivities), it is hardly surprising that many minority group parents will feel excluded, unacceptable, puzzled and even hostile towards their children's schools.

Staff-parent relationships and sensitivity to racial issues

At this point it is necessary to raise the question of whether one component of minority group parents' reluctance to take part in the life of the school is a suspicion that teachers are racially prejudiced. Very few teachers would admit to such prejudice, and indeed most would regard racist sentiments as morally wrong. But, despite this, teachers like the rest of society may display an insensitivity to the point of view of minority groups which can cause deep resentment. One example of this is the common use of the term 'coloured', with the implication that people of the most varied language, culture, and indeed, colour, can be grouped together by virtue of the fact that their skins are not 'white'.

Teachers may also be insensitive to the way in which minority groups are depicted in the school's story and textbooks. Because most of us have grown up with books and comics in which the 'white man' is portrayed as civilized and noble, the 'black man' as savage, primitive or comical, we tend not to think about the effects of these portrayals on black children's sense of identity. But West Indian and African parents do not view Little Black Sambo with affection. They are quick to notice if black people are depicted in the schools' books and pictorial material as semi-clothed savages living in huts, if people in Third World countries are generally depicted as in need of charity—the 'Oxfam image'—or if their children are taught that America and Africa were 'discovered' by Europeans.

Infants, and even nursery children, are frequently called 'wog' or 'paki' by white children, especially in the playground. Teachers often believe that this name-calling should not be taken too seriously, since it seems to them no more or less insulting than such taunts as 'four-eyes' or 'midget'. There is, however, good research evidence that by or even before the age of five both black and white children are well aware of the derogatory attitudes to minority groups held by much of society. To be called a 'wog' is not therefore simply perceived by the child and his parents as personally offensive, but reinforces their awareness of the hostility of the wider society towards their own group. For this reason staff need to have a clear policy, known to children and parents, for dealing with racist insults.

Some teachers who would not countenance racist insults claim that they are 'colour-blind', and treat all children in the same way. This policy, albeit carried out with a real concern to be fair, may in fact be damaging to black children, and appear to parents to be racist. This is because, while stating that 'all children are the same', the school in fact operates as though all children were white. The children, and their parents, see no recognition of themselves in the life of the school. To a large extent of course, this is even more true of society at large—black children in this country have to grow up in the knowledge that the cult-figures of childhood, whether spacemen, TV stars, or fairy-tale characters, are almost invariably white. Schools, however, have the opportunity to point out to both white and black children the contributions that have been made by many different cultures: they are in a position to develop a positive policy aimed to help all children towards an appreciation of, and respect for, ethnic, cultural and linguistic diversity.

A somewhat different problem is the tendency of some teachers to allow attitudes to individual children and their parents to be influenced by stereotypes about the characteristics of minority groups. Thus any negative features of the child may be 'explained' in terms of his own or his parents' group membership—for example, some teachers almost expect children of West Indian origin to be aggressive and to be low achievers. In consequence, factors in the school situation which might have a bearing on the child's poor behaviour or low achievements are overlooked. Or little effort may be made to discuss educational issues with Asian parents because they are believed to be illiterate, and uneducated, when a closer knowledge of the family might reveal their intense concern with their children's education. Any multi-cultural school which sets out to discuss these issues with its parents is likely to find the parents very aware of racial stereotypes, and anxious lest these stereotypes should prejudice the treatment of their children.

Ways of working with minority group parents

Aims

- To facilitate the contribution of minority group parents to the life of the school by adopting a multi-cultural approach

- To enable minority group parents to contribute their knowledge of their children and their culture to the teachers

- To enable teachers to consult minority group parents about their children's education, and discuss educational issues with them

- To help teachers to explain their aims and methods to minority group parents

In the course of our project we made some steps towards involving minority group parents in the life of the school. In one school, where two thirds of the parents were from minority groups, 80 per cent attended film shows about their children's activities at school. This attendance rate was achieved by repeating the films at hours to suit shift and night workers, giving parents information in their own language, and inviting them to bring other relatives. In the same class, mothers from a number of different cultures made illustrated books for the class, in their own languages, relating tales from their own childhood (see pages 194–7). An essential prerequisite for this contribution was probably the fact that the research officer concerned visited each family at home, explained how they could contribute and why it would be of value to the child and the school, brought the necessary materials, and discussed in detail with the family how to make the books and what might go in them. International social evenings also took place in this school.

In another project school, serving a largely Sikh population, individual appointments were made for mothers to visit the school and watch the class in action; mothers were invited to the school to make Asian sweets with the children; parents helped the school to celebrate Guru Nanak's birthday, and evening meetings at which the head explained the schools' aims and methods were attended by about 50 per cent of the families.

These steps were useful beginnings, but they often failed to achieve the aims for which they were set up. An occasional international social evening does not necessarily increase goodwill—it may instead confirm existing attitudes that the English are stand-offish, the West Indians noisy, that Asians eat 'peculiar' food, and so on. Nor is it enough to increase the numbers of parents going to school meetings, unless at such meetings parents freely put forward their own points of view. It cannot be assumed that because parents have spent time in the classroom they have understood or sympathized with what the teacher was trying to achieve. When we asked Asian mothers whether seeing what went on in school had helped them to understand the school better, 60 per cent of them said no. This was not because of the mothers' inability to understand, but because their attitudes to children, play, schools and education were very different from those of the staff. Unless teachers make determined efforts to understand these attitudes, consult the parents, and listen to their points of view, a parent involvement programme can leave teachers feeling very frustrated. It may seem to them that they have made considerable efforts, and that these have not been adequately appreciated by the parents.

This situation, like all those we have outlined above, is not peculiar to schools in multi-racial areas. It is also the case that many white indigenous working class parents are puzzled by 'learning through play' methods, find the concept of parent involvement unfamiliar, would like their children to make an early start with the 'three Rs', and find the culture of the school alien. (Compare the books, pictures, decoration and furnishings of a modern primary school with those chosen by working class parents in the locality for their own homes.) Moreover, just as teachers may have false and devaluing stereotypes about ethnic minority cultures, they may also believe that white working class parents have little to offer to the school.

Our interviews suggested, however, that these problems existed in a much more acute form in multi-cultural schools and that it was correspondingly more difficult to achieve any real teacher-parent partnership in these schools. For minority group parents to have the opportunity for full involvement—that is, to contribute their knowledge of their children and their cultures —and to be consulted about the way they are educated, radical changes would be necessary. The school would have to make exceptional efforts to respect, and to be seen to respect and understand, the cultures of the families it served. In effect, what would be required would be a bi-cultural or multi-cultural school.

The multi-cultural school

Staffing

If a school is to be truly multi-cultural, serious efforts need to be made to recruit a proportion of teaching staff from the minority groups concerned. There are several reasons why this step should be regarded as a priority. For teachers, an on-the-spot interpreter, who is also familiar with the child-rearing customs, culture, and religion of the families served by the school, is essential. Both parents and children are helped by the presence of staff who speak their language, and look familiar. At present, if minority group members are employed it is likely to be as welfare assistants, cleaners and caretakers rather than teachers or heads. But it is crucial that some of the more senior posts in the school are held by minority group members. This is because, while welfare assistants can do a useful job as interpreters, they are unlikely to influence the curriculum of the school. Further, it is important for the self respect of minority group children and their parents—and for the respect which indigenous teachers and children accord them—that minority group staff are not confined to low status positions.

In order to recruit adequate numbers of such staff, re-orientation courses may be necessary for minority group teachers originally trained overseas, to familiarize them with British teaching methods, and if necessary, to improve their command of English. Bridging courses, to help minority group leavers obtain the necessary qualifications to enter Colleges of Education, are of at least equal importance, and have already been organized in some areas.

Curriculum

The curriculum needs to be examined closely. Many schools do make attempts to move towards a multi-cultural curriculum. Usually, however, these moves take the form of adding multi-cultural 'touches' to current practice, or removing obvious racial bias, when what is required is a thorough-going re-think of the assumptions underlying the whole school practice. Material likely to reinforce prejudices or stereotypes must, of course, be discarded—for example, books which depict black people as 'savages'. But more positively, an effort needs to be made to see that minority group cultures are represented in the curriculum. For example, the books used in the school should be examined to see whether they reflect the cultural diversity of society. The school library should include a range of books in the languages represented in the school, and stories and folk tales from other cultures. There is also a great need for books which show people of minority groups in a positive light, doing normal everyday things in a realistic and local setting. Besides Asian and West Indian folk-tales, black children growing up in Britain need books about urban British children like themselves, with whom they can identify. It is equally important for white children to read books in which the characters depicted are ordinary black children living in Britain.

In nursery and infant classes, similar considerations arise in the choice of play materials—the dolls, dressing-up clothes, furniture, utensils and ornaments for the home-corner, and in the selection of musical instruments, dances, games and songs. Stories in the children's mother tongue should be available, at least in the form of tape recordings. The festivals celebrated should include those of minority groups within the school, as well as the traditional Christmas and Easter festivals. Pictures on the wall should depict children and adults from the minority cultures in the school, and the content of religious assemblies should show some acknowledgement that not all children in the school are Christian. In some primary schools, religious assemblies are used as an occasion to talk to children about the lives and contributions of great men and women. It is important that teachers should include black, Asian, Greek or Turkish heroes and heroines to be celebrated in this manner.

Admittedly, multi-cultural resources such as books and pictures are scarce. However, there is a growing number of groups and organizations now producing useful and interesting materials. Some teachers have found it helpful to work together to produce their own materials, developing themes and topics about the environment in which the children live. For example, such topics as where we live, homes, shops, the games we play, where people work, the food we eat, where we meet, can all be developed to encompass the diverse cultures of the neighbourhood. Teachers who have tried this approach have been surprised by the willing help they receive from parents and the local community. Photographs of the children in the school and their families can provide much needed multi-cultural visual displays. The scarcity of multi-cultural books for very young children can be made good by enlisting the aid of parents to write books about their own lives, and those of their children, illustrated by family photographs (see pages 194–7).

Organizing parent involvement

Teachers in multi-cultural schools will require basic information about the backgrounds and cultures of the children they are teaching. Courses in which teachers are told about 'the West Indian family' or 'Asian customs' often confirm and reinforce stereotypes, and the generalities purveyed may be misleading. Instead, teachers should try to get to know the individual families and communities they are serving. But this task will be easier if they are equipped with some information about the languages and cultures of the minority groups. There is a great need for brief yet accurate booklets about the different minority group cultures to be made available in every staffroom. In the absence of such material, teachers can turn to local community groups, to parents, and to the local community relations council for the information which they require.

But perhaps even more important than this background information is that the teacher should have certain basic information about each individual child in her class—for instance the correct form of their names, the religion, dietary and clothing practices of the family, and the languages spoken, read and written by the child, his parents and other family members. A suggested list of essential information will be found at the end of this chapter.

Teachers in possession of this information will be better placed to consider whether the organization of wider aspects of school life shows adequate respect for the parents' culture and way of life. An obvious example is the school kitchen—cheese or eggs may be provided as an alternative for children with particular dietary requirements, but could schools offer an international menu in which Asian, West Indian and Greek dishes are alternated with traditional British fare? Again, if wearing underclothes for PE causes anxiety to parents, can an alternative and acceptable form of garment be devised? Once teachers understand the value which some parents attach to cleanliness, they are likely to make special effort to see that children's clothes and hair are adequately protected during 'messy' activities.

A thorough re-thinking of this nature requires prolonged discussion amongst the staff of the school. A two-day 'teach-in' during the school holidays, which included discussions with the local multi-cultural advisor and representatives of local community groups and parents might be a necessary first step.

The contribution of parents in multi-cultural schools

There is an obvious and readily accessible source of help for schools who want to respond to the needs and reflect the culture of minority groups. In-service courses, special advisors and advanced diplomas for teachers are important but the children's parents and the local community leaders can also advise the staff about educational aims, religion, customs, festivals, stories, music, food, games and decorative materials. The undoubted fact that at present minority group parents tend to stay away from schools reflects, in our opinion, the parents' belief that they cannot contribute to their children's education, and also that they are often unsympathetic to the school's approach. But how many heads and class teachers have asked these parents for help in contributing to the curriculum and in making the school truly multi-cultural, or have consulted with them about whether the school is meeting the needs of their children?

Our experience in one multi-cultural nursery class was that, when personal relationships had been established with the parents by visiting them in their homes and seeking their views on education, they enjoyed contributing their own experience to the classroom by writing or telling stories about their childhood, and the teacher was delighted with the result. But in order to forge real links with the community, it seems likely that teachers must make the first move, by going out of their school—visiting the children at home, using the local shops and cafés. They could ask for invitations to visit the families' churches, temples, and social centres, and discuss the possibility of holding school meetings and exhibitions in them. Teachers are often understandably nervous about establishing links with what seems to them a very alien culture, and sometimes find the initial steps easier with the support of one or two colleagues. (A similar nervousness is often felt by parents when visiting schools.)

It is, perhaps, important to point out that home visiting, like any work with parents, does not necessarily result in improved parent-teacher relationships—its effectiveness depends on how and why it's done. There is a danger that home visiting by teachers can become a form of social work, from which the teacher returns mainly impressed by the absence of toys and books in the home, or the evident difficulties in the lives of the parents. Such visits would not lead to an increased contribution by minority groups to the school, or to an increased respect by the teachers for the families, and could even be counterproductive. For this reason home visiting, in our opinion, should be arranged with specific educational aims—to discuss a child's progress at school, and to seek information and help from the parents (see pages 130–3). It should also be seen as one among many ways in which teachers move out towards the community.

As well as trying to get to know individual families, there is much to be said for an additional way of establishing links with parents, in which the parent body is approached as a group. This is certainly feasible in a school with a substantial number of children from one minority group. Representatives of minority group parents, staff and other members of the community can form a group to look at all aspects of school life, to help promote a multi-cultural approach, and to help the school explain its aims to the minority groups and respond to their needs. If the group concerned is non-English speaking, it can undertake other functions—for instance arrange for interpreters and translators, and classes for parents to learn English and for teachers to learn the minority languages.

Areas of conflict between staff and parents

Open discussion between staff and parents is likely to reveal the kind of disagreements on aims and methods which have already been outlined. Two other areas of potential disagreement between teachers and minority group parents are the role of punishment in the school, and the amount of emphasis that should be given to formal teaching.

We do not underestimate the difficulty of explaining modern teaching aims and methods to parents from a very different culture. Nor do we suggest that teachers should—or indeed would—accede to parental wishes which were totally at variance with their own approach. But unless schools are prepared to discuss such issues with parents, explain their approach, listen to the parents' points of view, and go some way towards meeting them, they cannot hope to enlist parental support for their work. Teachers might think it worth considering whether, because of their intimate knowledge of a child and his environment, his parents' opinions about his educational needs should be taken seriously. For instance, if parents are worried because 'modern maths' seems to have superceded mental arithmetic, a teacher might consider supplementing her mathematics curriculum with mental arithmetic, or showing parents how they can help their child to learn it at home.

The objections of parents to sand and water play may disappear if they receive an adequate explanation of why the teacher considers the materials important, especially if the children are provided with suitable protective clothing—like hats for sand play, and waterproof overalls for water play. Alternatively, the teacher may decide in the face of entrenched parental objections that sand and water play are not educational essentials. If parents are concerned that their children are not being taught English systematically at school, the staff may have a fresh look at what is known about second language teaching for young children, and the comparative effectiveness of different methods.

Organizing parent involvement

It is not, of course, likely that one meeting or discussion with parents will be very effective in improving mutual understanding. This is only likely to develop over a period of time, in which teachers have shown in a variety of ways that they respect the parents' culture, want to listen to their opinions, and are willing to take their points of view seriously.

Mother tongue teaching

A difficult and controversial question is that of whether the school should undertake mother tongue teaching, both oral and written, for children from other cultures. Many minority group communities organize 'supplementary' schools for this purpose, and they may well prefer to undertake the teaching of their own language and culture themselves. But it could be argued that a multi-cultural school, particularly in an area with a high concentration of families from one culture, should be bilingual, or at least advance all the children's education in both cultures. Such a policy would, of course, require the employment of a substantial proportion of minority group staff. It would certainly seem appropriate to raise these issues with parent groups, since they are ones of deep concern to many minority group parents.

It would also seem important to discuss with parents whose native language is not English the question of the best language to use with their children at home. We have found that some parents, anxious to help their children's education, speak to them only in English, even when their own command of the language is poor. Teachers need to be aware of this practice, and its possible disadvantages for the children, and discuss the question with parents.

The language barrier

For many teachers in multi-cultural areas the most easily identified problem in working with parents is 'the language barrier'. This problem could be considerably eased by a local authority's determination to employ members of the minority groups on the staff, or to employ interpreters for schools, or to assist any English staff who wanted to learn the minority languages. In a school where the children spoke many languages, their situation would be eased if there were at least one teacher who had some knowledge of each minority language. At a much less ambitious level, we have found that parents are very appreciative if a teacher makes the effort to learn to greet them in their own language.

Where funds are not available for interpreters, and minority group members are not on the staff, we have a number of suggestions to offer which involve making the best use of the resources that are at present available.

Interpreters and translators

Whether a school has only one parent with whom communication in English presents problems, or whether it has 90 per cent, an interpreter should be available to both parents and staff. Often some member of the family, even an older child, can play this role; it is not a good idea to rely on other parents to interpret (though it may occasionally be necessary) because of considerations of confidentiality. Local minority groups may be able to supply interpreters, if the school has made efforts to be involved in these groups. Resentment can easily be built up when schools appear to be restricting their contact with minority group agencies and organizations to the occasions when they require a service from them. On the other hand, in an atmosphere of mutual respect and goodwill, much help may be forthcoming.

For translations of prospectuses, newsletters and notices

similar sources of help, including parents, can be used. Parents will be especially helpful in examining materials for appropriate content relevant to their cultures, checking that dates do not clash with a religious celebration, and that the information given covers points which parents are likely to be concerned about.

Holding meetings for parents who do not speak English presents schools with a rather greater problem than finding interpreters for day-to-day individual conversation. The obvious approach is to have translators available at meetings to translate sequentially what is said. But this is inevitably obtrusive, difficult, and time consuming, and prevents the natural flow of discussion. In schools where at least two languages are spoken by large numbers of parents one solution is to provide the same meeting separately for the different language groups. This is at first sight a divisive practice, but if the main priority is for communication to take place between staff and parents then it may be acceptable as the only solution. Opportunities for all parents in the school to get together may be more appropriately provided by less verbal occasions—such as socials, outings, picnics, or concerts.

Another approach is to suggest that parents organize for themselves bilingual representatives who can mediate between staff and their language group. Parents can then approach the school through the bilingual committee, suggesting topics for meetings and arranging interpreters. The committees can meet as a group to discuss and report to all other parents about meetings held, discussions, decisions and so forth.

Commentaries for films can obviously be made in the required languages and shown at different times to parents speaking different languages. Reports can be kept of discussions, and a meeting held for all parents when questions and answers could be given, using interpreters.

Evaluation

● We cannot offer a ready made list of points for evaluation, because the suggestions we have made have been general, rather than specific. The kind of questions which teachers in multi-cultural schools might consider in evaluating their work with parents could include 'What proportion of parents from minority groups attend school functions? How many staff have spent time in the neighbourhood visiting the churches, temples, shops, and cafes frequented by minority group parents? Has school practice and school curriculum been modified as a result of discussion with minority group parents?'

Suggested essential information for teachers working with minority group parents and children

Information about the child and his family

Names of children and members of family; the form of name by which each should be addressed

Country of origin, and region, of parents

Religion

Dietary, clothing, and other practices of the family which will affect provisions made in school

The mother tongue of the parents; other languages spoken/read/written by parents and other family members. The language used between parents and children

The language to be used in communication between home and school

The form communications should take—spoken or written

If an interpreter from outside the family is necessary, his name and how to contact him

Organizing parent involvement

Essential information for the staffroom

(Parents and other members of the community may give helpful advice, and add more specific local information)

Books and pamphlets on the religions, cultures, countries/ regions represented in school

Names and addresses of local community leaders, groups, etc.

Details of religious meeting places, dates of festivals and their meanings

Names and addresses of interpreters available, and translators

Maps and charts indicating countries and areas of origin of parents in school, their languages, dialects and religions

Bibliographies and addresses of organizations where more information can be obtained

References and name index

BASSEY, M. (1978) *Nine hundred Primary School Teachers*. London: NFER. *31*

BERNSTEIN, B. (1970) Education cannot compensate for society. *New Society* **387**, 344–7, 26 February. *13*

BERNSTEIN, B. (1971) *Class Codes and Control*. Vol. 1. London: Routledge & Kegan Paul. *13*

BERNSTEIN, B., and DAVIES, B. (1969) Some sociological comments on Plowden. In Peters, R. S. (ed.) *Perspectives on Plowden*. London: Routledge & Kegan Paul. *11*

BLANK, M. (1973) *Teaching Learning in the Pre-school*. Columbus, Ohio: Charles E. Merrill. *13*

BLOOM, B. S. (1964) *Stability and Change in Human Characteristics*. New York and Chichester: Wiley. *14*

BOWLBY, J. (1951) *Maternal Care and Mental Health*. Geneva: World Health Organization. *7, 14*

BRONFENBRENNER, U. (1974) *A Report on Longitudinal Evaluations of Pre-school Programs*. Vol. 2. US Department of Health, Education and Welfare Publication No. OH D 72-74. *35*

BRUNER, J. S. (1974) *Beyond the Information given*. New York: Norton; London: Allen & Unwin. *13*

BULLOCK REPORT (1975) *A Language for Life*. London: HMSO. *12, 16, passim*

CLARKE, A. M., and CLARKE, A. D. B. (1976) *Early Experience: Myth and Evidence*. London: Open Books; New York: Free Press. *15*

CONNOLLY, K. J. (1972) Learning and the concept of critical periods in infancy. *Development and Child Neurology* **14**, 705–14. *14*

CROWTHER REPORT (1959) *Report of the Central Advisory Council for Education*. **15–18**, England: HMSO. *8*

References and name index

DONACHY, W., and CLARK, M. (1979) *Studies in Pre-school Education.* London: Hodder & Stoughton. *27*

DOUGLAS, J. W. B. (1964) *The Home and the School.* London: Macgibbon & Kee. *8, 10*

EARLY LEAVING (1954) Report of the Central Advisory Council for Education. London: HMSO. *8*

GARVEY, A. (1975) Belfield Community School Rochdale. *Where?* **102**. March. *111*

FRANCIS, H. (1974) Social background, speech, and learning to read. *British Journal of Educational Psychology* **44**, 290–9. *13*

HALSEY, A. H. (ed.) (1972) *Educational Priority.* Vol. 1. London: HMSO. *15, passim*

HEWISON, J. (1981) Home is where the help is. *The Times Educational Supplement* **3369**, 20. 16 January.

HUGHES, M., MAYALL, B., MOSS, P., PERRY, J., PETRIE, P., and PINKERTON, G. (1980) *Nurseries Now.* Harmondsworth: Penguin. *20*

JACKSON, B., and MARSDEN, D. (1962) *Education and the Working Class,* Harmondsworth: Penguin. *9, passim*

JENSEN, A. R. (1969) How much can we boost IQ and scholastic achievement? *Harvard Educational Review* **39**, 1–123. *14*

LAZAR, I., HUBBELL, V. V., MURRAY, H., ROSCHE, M., and ROYCE, T. (1977) *The persistence of pre-school effects: a long-term follow up of 14 infant and pre-school experiments.* US Department of Health, Education and Welfare. *35*

MCMILLAN, M. A bibliography can be found in Bradbury, E. (1976) *Margaret McMillan* Redhill, Surrey: Denholm House Press. *28, 29, passim*

MIDWINTER, E. (1972) *Priority Education.* Harmondsworth: Penguin. *25*

MIDWINTER, E. (1977) *Education for Sale.* London: Allen & Unwin. *9, 25*

NATIONAL UNION OF TEACHERS (1979) *Parents in Schools.* Policy Document. London: NUT. *34*

NEWSOM REPORT (1963) *Half our Future.* Central Advisory Council for Education. London: HMSO. *8*

NEWSON, J., and NEWSON, E. (1977) *Perspectives on School at Seven Years Old.* London: George Allen and Unwin. *12, 31, 107*

PLOWDEN REPORT (1967) *Children and their Primary Schools.* Central Advisory Council for Education. London: HMSO. *7, 10, 23, passim*

SMITH, T. (1980) *Parents and Preschool.* London: Grant McIntyre. *36*

TIZARD, B., CARMICHAEL, H., HUGHES, M., and PINKERTON, G. (1980) Four Year olds Talking to Mothers and Teachers.

In Hersov, L. A., Berger, M., and Nicoll, A. R. (eds.) *Language and Language Disorders in Childhood*. Book supplement to the *Journal of Child Psychology and Psychiatry* No. 2. *13*

TOUGH, J. (1976) *The Development of Meaning: A Study of Children's Use of Language*. London: Allen & Unwin. *13*

TOUGH, J. (1977) *Talking and Learning*. London: Ward Lock Educational. *34*

WATT, J. (1977) *Cooperation in Pre-School Education*. London: SSRC. *32*

WOOTTON, A. (1974) Talk in the homes of young children. *Sociology* **8**, 277. *13*

YOUNG, M., and MCGEENEY, P. (1968) *Leaving Begins at Home*. London: Routledge & Kegan Paul. *9, 35*

Subject Index

Index